For five hundred years the Lucas family have been part of Gower history. The land was in their blood. They farmed it, married for it, mined it, studied its rich wild life, and sometimes left it – for the Grand Tour or adventures at sea – yet always returned. Tradition tells of a darker side; murder, piracy and wrecking on the wild Gower coast.

Here now is the true story. With lively scholarship and in elegant prose Robert Lucas reassesses the legends and traces his forbears from their distant yeoman origins at Stouthall, through the Palladian grace of the 18th century to more recent frugal days at the lonely parsonage at Rhosili. The family letters, deeds and diaries over the centuries bring alive the clamour of everyday life, and from the dusty archives emerge fascinating pen portraits of the writer's ancestors, making their diverse and colourful contribution to the history of this lovely part of Wales.

Robert Lucas is the President of the Gower Society. He has published many articles on Lucas and Gower history in its annual journal, and has lectured widely on the subject.

A graduate of St John's College, Oxford, he was in the army at the outbreak of war. Reaching the rank of Major he served with distinction in France and Burma – when he trekked across the Himalayas into Tibet in the spirit of his adventurous forbears. After the war he was for many years in practice as a country Solicitor at Saffron Walden near Cambridge, and now lives at Reynoldston, the traditional family home on the Gower peninsula in South Wales.

Besides his interest in local history he is a keen gardener and photographer and local Community Councillor. He is married with two children.

John Lucas the younger, c. 1775

A GOWER
FAMILY

THE LUCASES OF
STOUTHALL
AND
RHOSILI RECTORY

by
$\underline{ROBERT\ LUCAS}$

The Book Guild Limited

For the grandchildren

The Book Guild Limited
Temple House
25 High Street
Lewes, Sussex
First published 1986
© Robert Lucas 1986
Printed in Great Britain by
Antony Rowe Ltd.,
Chippenham, Wilts

ISBN 0 86332 126 7

Contents

List of Illustrations

Preface

I was brought up to believe that my Gower forebears were smugglers and pirates, descended from an ancient family of East Anglian aristocrats, whose ancestor came over with William the Conqueror. There were two family heroes. One was Sir Charles Lucas, a Cavalier who fought and died for King Charles in the Civil War; the other was John Lucas, pirate and outlaw, a kind of Gower Robin Hood who operated from the Salt House at Porteynon. The principal source of information about these romantic characters and about the family in general has hitherto been my father's scrap book, a fascinating family medley which I greatly treasure, but in which fact, fiction and surmise are confusingly jumbled. The present book is an attempt to tell the true story and if the traditions are left looking a little shaky I hope no-one is going to be too disappointed.

All families with any history must have a pedigree and this being Wales we have plenty of them, pushed into bookcases and stacked away in odd corners — formidable family trees on enormous pieces of paper fit to be proudly unrolled on the sitting room carpet. Most of them are unreliable, and for the Stouthall pedigree I have had to start again at the beginning. Unfortunately the economics of book production have made it impossible to include more than the outline pedigree to be found on page 172, and the same applies, regrettably, to many of the detailed notes and references which support the facts given in the book. These are available separately as explained in the author's note on page 173/4.

There is a particular difficulty in writing about the Lucases which must be common to all families of insufficient importance to have attracted independent comment from their contemporaries. The letters and personal papers which have survived tend to be those which fond relatives thought at the time to be worth keeping. So a form of censorship, deliberate or unconscious, must be assumed to have taken place, and often we have nothing else to go by. Has Grandmama perhaps, in the nicest possible way, pulled the wool a little over our eyes? It is a question we have to ask, as we gently finger the dried posies of sea pinks, the faded photographs, and those poignant little locks of silky hair, snipped from the heads of infants and the unburied dead. I make no apology for a few digressions about people and places where these seem to have become woven in to the family story. I know that to digress is to embark on a slippery slope, and only hope I have kept my balance better than the late E. E. Rowse who in his guide book entitled *In and Around Swansea* managed to slip in four chapters on 'The Discourses of Paul the Apostle Imprisoned in Rome'.

A book about the Lucases at Stouthall and Rhosili is inevitably a book about Gower. It tells of a family devoted to their homeland in this wind-swept corner of Wales, and of some peculiar social attitudes which flourished in the isolation of Rhosili Rectory. If in writing about my forefathers I have been able here and there to shed a little light on these aspects of a vanished world it may be of interest beyond the family circle.

I owe thanks to a number of people: to Mr R. C. B. Oliver and Major Francis Jones, TD, CVO, for some help with pedigrees; to John and Barbara Barratt for the loan of their invaluable collection of family documents; to Mrs Iris Adams, Mrs Letty Harcourt-Tepper and Miss May Laidlaw for showing me their family pictures and albums and for much good family talk; to Mr Michael Gibbs, Mr W. C. Rogers and Dr Prys Morgan for helping me with their expert knowledge of Gower and Welsh families and houses, and to Mr M. C. S. Evans for the loan of a contemporary account of the trial of William Spiggott and others at Hereford Assizes in 1770. I am particularly grateful to Mr David Bevan, archivist at the University College of Swansea, to Dr Joanna Martin for her notes on 18th and 19th century deeds and to the Editorial Board of the Gower Society in whose journal parts of this book have already appeared. I thank the Royal Institution of South Wales and the University College of Swansea for permission to quote from the journal of W. H. Essery and the diaries of the Reverend John Collins. Some sources which I have found particularly helpful I have listed by way of acknowledgment at the end of the book.

The account of Stouthall in the 1890s by the late Mr C. E. Vulliamy, part of which is quoted in Chapter 8, appeared in the 1960 edition of *Gower*. I have tried unsuccessfully to trace his family and trust they will approve this quotation about a house which Mr Vulliamy held in great affection. The extract from John Masefield's *The Conway* is quoted with permission of his literary executor. The picture of the ship *Middlesex* is from a painting by the late Mr J. Spurling and I have to thank Mr Harold Grenfell, FRPS for permission to reproduce the photographs of Rhosili Rectory. In the preparation of this book, as in many other things, I have relied on my wife for encouragement and wise counsel.

Lastly I must acknowledge the debt owed to my father Captain Loftus Lucas and to my sister Catherine. To Loftus for much painstaking research and for assembling a vast and delightful treasure store in his famous scrap book; to Catherine who, after years of devoted caring for aunt May, the last surviving daughter of the Reverend J. P. Lucas of Rhosili, had the task of sorting a lifetime's accumulation of papers in that bleak cold flat in West Hampstead. Had it not been for Catherine's keen and scholarly eye so many relics of a Gower family would have found their way into the dustbin.

REYNOLDSTON 1984

Outline Pedigree —
Lucases of Stouthall

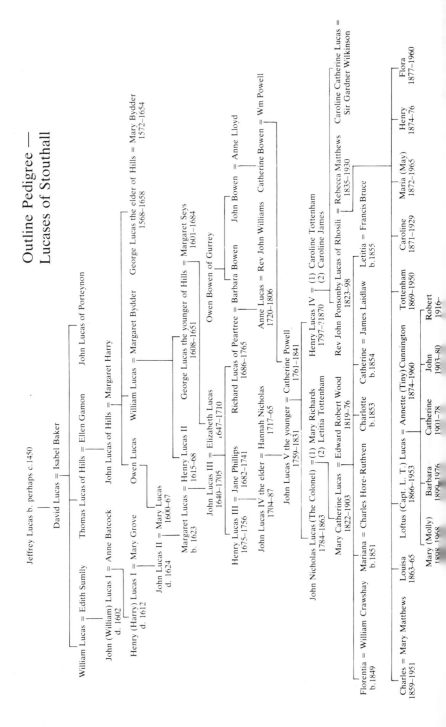

1

1485–1750
The Reynoldston Farmers

The Lucas family have been living in the Gower peninsula in south-west Wales for at least 500 years. We can trace them back to one Jeffrey Lucas who lived probably in Reynoldston Parish during the second half of the 15th century. Jeffrey is not a common Gower name and it never reappears in the family. This suggests that Jeffrey may have come to Gower from elsewhere, and that he was not a person of enough importance for his descendants to take any special pride in his first name. The family flourished as yeoman farmers and minor gentry during the 16th and 17th centuries, and by the early 1700s the Reynoldston branch of the family had attained a dominant position as squires and landowners in west Gower.

The south and west of the Gower peninsula is English by tradition and has been so since the arrival of the Normans nearly 900 years ago. These early Norman conquerors very likely came by sea from across the Bristol Channel. English settlers were introduced, the Welsh driven out, and almost all trace of the indigenous Welsh culture disappeared. This area became known as English Gower. With its fertile limestone valleys and cliff land and its mild climate English Gower was first-rate farmland and the early settlers prospered whenever political conditions were sufficiently stable for them to do so. To the north and east was Welsh Gower, which extended out of the peninsula to the north of Swansea and up into the high country lying between the valleys of the Tawe and Llwchwr rivers. Here the scattered communities retained their Welsh language and their age-old traditions. The whole of Gower, English and Welsh, became under the Normans what was known as a Marcher Lordship, where the Norman overlord, although a liege subject of the King of England, held almost absolute power.

After the victory of Henry Tudor, to be crowned King Henry VII, at Bosworth field in 1485 Welshmen rose to positions of power at the English Court, and among the landowning and gentry classes in South Wales in Tudor times to be English was to be in the fashion. The Acts of Union in the 1530s whereby the Marcher Lordships were abolished and the English shires set up in their place were welcomed by English and Welsh alike. It is during this period, the middle of the 16th century, that we begin to find contemporary documents referring to Lucases in Gower. During the next hundred years there are so many references to them in title deeds and manorial documents that one can only conclude that at almost every farm in west Gower the children, playing in the summer hayfields or lying awake on a still winter's night listening to the roar of the surf, would have had Lucas uncles, aunts or cousins if they did not have Lucas parents. Where did the Lucases come from? It has become the accepted tradition that they came to Gower from East Anglia during the 15th century. We can trace this tradition back as far as 1687 when John Lucas III of Stouthall used the coat of arms of the Lucases of Essex and Suffolk; and his descendants have made use of it ever since, although without authority from the College of Heralds. These East Anglian Lucases played a prominent part in public affairs during the time of the Wars of the Roses, the Tudor period, and the Civil War, but there is no known link to connect them with the yeoman farmers and gentry of Gower. Did John III perhaps know of some link, now forgotten, when he had their coat of arms engraved on his seal during the second half of the 17th century? Possibly, but not necessarily so. It was not uncommon for the emerging gentry families to improve their status by adopting a coat of arms to which they were not strictly entitled. When Charles II was restored to the throne in 1660, John was a young man of 20. His East Anglian namesakes had become famous for the sacrifices they had made in the Royalist cause. The cavalry leader Sir Charles Lucas had defended Colchester for the King, and been shot by Fairfax for his pains. His brother Thomas had died of wounds in Ireland fighting for the Royalist cause. Another brother had been ennobled as Lord Lucas of Shenfield; and their sister Margaret was married to the great Duke of Newcastle. With her literary flair and eccentricity she was the talk of London town. Would it be unfair to suggest that in the heady Royalist atmosphere of the 1660s young John Lucas of Stouthall in Gower may have felt it unnecessary to do much historical research before hitching his waggon to such a fashionable team?

If we are to look elsewhere than East Anglia for the family origin the obvious places would be Wales and the West Country. Although Lucas is not a common name in Wales we do find a few Lucases in and around Gower in early medieval times so the Gower connection may go back even further than is generally supposed. There were also Lucases in the West Country in early times when the trading links with the Gower peninsula no doubt encouraged many a West Countryman to seek his fortune, and perhaps a wife too, on the opposite side of the Bristol Channel. Might there perhaps have been some link with those sea-faring Lucases living round the Tamar estuary since the 15th century (one of them was a pirate) some of whose latter day 19th century descendants (farming people) lie in Morwenstow churchyard on the cruel North Cornish coast? It is pure conjecture, but we need not look so far afield as East Anglia for our origins.

The Lucases of west Gower in late Tudor times are well documented. Besides the Penrice and Margam manuscripts now in the National Library of Wales there is a valuable collection of Gower pedigrees compiled by William Bennett of Penrice Castle farm who died in about 1642. These pedigrees are in the library of the University College of Swansea, and are thought by scholars to be accurate. Bennett starts with Jeffrey Lucas but says nothing about his origins. He traces three branches of Jeffrey's descendants. Jeffrey's son David of Reynoldston who married Isabel Baker of Oxwich had three sons, probably born during the early years of the 16th century. John the eldest went to Porteynon. Contemporary records of this Porteynon branch are scanty. John and his descendants disappear into obscurity, to re-emerge in a rather startling manner some 400 years later. How this came about, and how John has now become a Gower folk hero, the notorious outlaw smuggler and pirate of Porteynon, will be told in a later chapter. William, the second son of David and Isabel, settled at Stouthall in Reynoldston Parish, and Thomas the third son went to Hills farm also in Reynoldston. By the middle years of the reign of Queen Elizabeth I both the Stouthall and Hills branches were well-established farming families. Thomas was also a musician of some note whose playing of the Welsh crwth — an early form of violin — was remembered in Gower for 100 years after his death.

Four of Thomas Lucas's ten children married into the Welsh family of Harri. Owain Harry or ap Harri came from Llanelli and his wife Maud was a Gower woman. One of their sons, George Owen Harry, became a clergyman and married Thomas Lucas's daughter Ann. He became Vicar of Whitchurch in Pembrokeshire and a close friend of the celebrated historian and antiquary, also named George Owen, who lived in the neighbouring Parish of Henllys. George Owen Harry (he confusingly dropped the Harry but I keep it to distinguish him from his friend) became a notable calligraphist and genealogist. The construction of Welsh pedigrees had previously been the province of the bards, but in Elizabethan times it was becoming the hobby of country gentlemen. The art of genealogy still retained much of its bardic and legendary quality as is evident from the title of George Owen Harry's major work composed in 1604 — *The Wellspring of True Nobilitie. The Genealogy of the High and Mightye Monarch James . . . King of Great Brittayne Etc with His Lineall Descent from Noah, by Divers Direct Lines to Brutus.* If George Owen Harry ever wrote up his wife's pedigree it has not survived, so we are unable to make what might have been a fascinating backward journey from the Lucases of Reynoldston to Noah.

Thomas Lucas's eldest son John married a Harry daughter, and their eldest son George (1568–1658) married Mary Bydder of Highway in Pennard Parish. This George Lucas 'the elder' of Hills owned some 265 acres in Reynoldston and many other Gower properties from Swansea to Rhosili. By contrast the Stouthall Lucases at this time seem to have owned no more than about 32 acres of freehold with a further 48 acres on lease in Reynoldston, as well as some other properties elsewhere in Gower. The period covered by the lifespan of George Lucas the elder was a time of prosperity for the Gower farmers. Reynoldston was good corn ground and noted for its crops of wheat, barley, rye, oats, peas and vetches. Livestock, corn and wool were exported from the little ports of Oxwich and Porteynon to Barnstaple and Ilfracombe and elsewhere. The Lord of the Manor provided the port facilities and collected the harbour dues, twopence for a horse, a farthing for a sheep and a halfpenny for a hog.

The ownership and occupation of land was based on the Manorial system. Most of the Gower Manors including Reynoldston were 'old knights' fees' in which the Lord of the Manor in medieval times held his land from the Lord of Gower in return for military service, and made similar demands on his tenants. By the close of the Tudor period this aspect of feudalism was almost obsolete, but as late as

1603 Harry Lucas of Stouthall rented 8 acres in Penrice from Sir Thomas Mansel at a rent of 20 marks, the tenants to be 'retainers or bearers of weapons in any matter touching Sir Thomas Mansel'. Usually the customary freeholders paid rents and services which were no more than nominal, and in some cases picturesque. For their 178 acres of freehold land in Reynoldston the Lucases of Stouthall and Hills paid a yearly rent of about one halfpenny per acre. For a 5-acre field called Sladacres in Penrice in 1632 David Lucas's rent was a 'redd rose at midsomer'.

Apart from the fortunate few with their customary freeholds most landowners held on a lease for lives from the Lord of the Manor at a rent which in a time of rapidly rising land values soon dropped well below the real value of the land.

The lease for three lives was a system which continued well into the 19th century. It was usual to choose the lives of the farmer and his wife and one of their children, the younger the better from the tenant's point of view; although to choose the life of a very young child must have been rather a gamble in the days of high infant mortality. On the death of a 'life' application was often made to the landlord to include a fresh life but this gave the landlord an opportunity to raise the rent and to demand payment of a premium which might be substantial.

Stouthall in early Stuart times was held by the Lucases on a lease for lives granted to them by the overlord of Gower William Herbert Earl of Pembroke. This house, which became the principal family home, bore no resemblance to the present house which was not built until the end of the 18th century. The old Stouthall stood between the site of the present house and the South Gower road. Nothing now remains of it except the old well which probably served the original house and may be found among the trees between the west end of the present mansion and the road. There is reason to think that old Stouthall was similar in appearance to Pitt farmhouse in Oxwich which still stands and is outwardly much the same as when it was built in about 1600. In 1670 Pitt, with eight hearths, and Stouthall and Hills with seven each, were among the largest houses in the Gower peninsula. The origin of the name Stouthall is uncertain. It has been suggested that it was originally Stoutwalls, a version which appears in an 18th century note on William Bennett's pedigree. The earliest known reference to the house is in a deed of grant in 1583 in favour of 'Johani Lucas de Stouthole yeoman'. The versions Stowthall and Stothall appear early in the 17th century, and one cannot draw any firm conclusion from the spelling vagaries of the early lawyers' clerks. It is quite likely that the name was originally Stout Hole or Stot Hole. Hole farm is a familiar Gower placename, and may refer to one of the numerous holes or sinks into which Gower streams have a habit of disappearing underground. There is an example close to Stouthall.

The John Lucas referred to in the deed of 1583, John I, had three sons, Harry, David and George. Harry inherited Stouthall. John I bought a property for David at Capons or Galpens Hill in Penrice parish. This house which still existed in 1783 but was later demolished stood on a hillside about a quarter of a mile west of Penrice water mill which was at the bottom of the hill known as Penny Hitch. The site of the house, on the west side of a small lake, is now under woodland. It was a simple single storey house, probably with a thatched roof, and contained no more than two rooms, the Hall which was the living room, and the Chamber which served as a bedroom for David and his wife Mary Beynon. Their two children probably slept in an attic. Adjoining the house were the stall houses for the beasts, and a barn. There was a herb garden by the south window. David's farm was 48 acres of which 12 were freehold and the rest held on a lease for lives. This was probably a typical farmhouse for the middling sort of Gower farmer in the 17th century. Often the Chamber was no more than an extension on the side of the house, the bed outshut or 'cupboard bed' which was a special feature of Gower farmhouses.

When David's brother Harry died at Stouthall in 1612 the family made an inventory and valuation of his goods and chattels:

An inventory of the goods and cattles of Harry Lukas deceased prysed by George Lukas Rowland Bydder David Lukas Lewys Thomas David Batcocke and Thomas Lukas

	£	s	d
9 oxen	12	0	0
22 kyne (dairy cows)	22	0	0
2 three year old bullocks	1	6	8
Two year old bullocks	2	10	0
8 twelve month old bullocks	2	0	0
7 calves of this year	0	14	0

11 horses mares and coltes	5	0	0
116 wethers ewes and lambs	13	0	0
11 swine greate and small	1	0	0
poultry	0	5	0
The thirde part of a lease for certain years to come	4	0	0
6 acres wheate in the ground	4	0	0
8 acres otes in the ground	4	0	0
5 acres barley	3	0	0
Mow in otes on another man's lande	1	0	0
Corne of all kind being in the house and haggard	4	0	0
plough stuffe and harrowes	0	6	8
household stuffe as brasses pewters and other implements	10	0	0
plate	2	0	0
	92	2	4
debts due to the testator	3	14	5
sum total	95	16	9

The oxen were used mainly as draught animals, particularly for ploughing. There were few Gower farmers who owned more than six of them. The next most valuable livestock were the dairy cows. The horses were used for general farm work. They were often bred for sale and shipped across the Bristol Channel. Wool, wheat and butter also went for export, and Gower butter was noted for its fine quality. Pigs, surprisingly, seem to have been kept mainly by the better-off farmers, although by the 19th century almost every cottager had a pig or two. The hens and cockerels were worth about threepence each. It has been estimated that a substantial farmer, by Gower standards, was worth between £50 and £60 at this period, so Harry Lucas at around £90 must have been farming on a larger scale than most of his neighbours. The item 'plate' in Harry's inventory, which means silver, shows that the family already had some cherished possessions. Harry had six children of whom all but the eldest, John, were under 21 when he died. The five younger ones were each left sums of money, £25 or £30, to be inherited at 21, and meanwhile they were to receive under the terms of the will 'meate drinke and apparrell for borde and bedd'. Harry bequeathed to his aged mother an annuity of 20 shillings 'and that she shall have her chafer [warming pan] a feather bedd a boulster a paire of blankets and a coverlet'.

Nothing is said about the land in Harry's will, because until quite recent times a man's land passed direct to his eldest son unless some special provision was made to the contrary. This had been the case in Gower from the early Norman times and enabled family estates to pass undiminished from one generation to the next, in contrast to the old Welsh system which treated all the sons equally, and led to the diminution and impoverishment of farms. From the end of the 17th century the devolution of land was commonly dealt with not in wills but in legal settlements drawn up on the marriage of the eldest son. The result was that the farmer's main wealth, his land, is seldom mentioned in his will.

A problem already apparent in the 17th century was the failure of male heirs, and the Lucas estates in Reynoldston only survived as a result of frequent intermarriage between the Hills and Stouthall families. The Hills branch of the family achieved an important advancement in their social status when George the elder arranged a marriage between his nephew George the younger — who was also his adopted son — and Margaret the daughter of Richard Seys, a member of a well-known gentry family from Boverton in the Vale of Glamorgan. This was a prestigious alliance, for the bride's grandfather Roger Seys had been Attorney General for Wales and her grandmother a Maid of Honour to Queen Elizabeth. Evan Seys, the bride's uncle, was a distinguished lawyer and antiquary. This Seys connection became a close one, and from it may have stemmed a certain bookishness and respect for academic distinction which persisted among the Lucases.

Although by the middle of the 17th century the more well-to-do members of the family would leave money to their children rather than goods and provide for their education during minority, in general a Gower farmer's concern, when he came to make his will, would be with his beasts and the contents of his house and farmyard. We have already seen the simple provision which Harry Lucas made for his mother. Nicholas Lucas of Oxwich in 1645 gives his mother half a stone of wool; and his eldest son is to have a capital sum of £10 at the age of 15 and 'one cupboord one taible and one greate crock after his mother's days'. The poor of the Parish would often be given a bushel of barley, and a servant a peck of barley. John Lucas of Knelston (1683) a yeoman farmer bequeathed to his daughter Margaret 'the white horn cow and one heifer and the use of the great pann during her life'. His nephew Roger Gibb was to have 'the great black cow' and nephew Samuel Jones '£5 and the pink horn cow'. To his sister Joan he left 'two bushalls of barly and one peck of wheat' yearly for her life, to be paid to her quarterly by equal portions; and three pounds of 'woolle of white and black' to be paid at May next after his death. His servant maid Margaret Grove was to receive 'one ewe and lamb'.

Lower down the social scale was yet another George Lucas who died in 1677/8. He was a bachelor and lived with his mother at the Western house in Reynoldston. He seems to have been a carpenter and perhaps the village undertaker as well. He was a man of few possessions, the most important of which he bequeathed as follows: 'I give to my cozen Mary Price my young mare; I give to Nicholas Hugh all my carpenter tooles and a coat and britches and alsoe fower plancks of elme; I give to Griffith Morris a coate and britches and paire of shooes and a wastcoate; I give to Owen Russell a coate and britches wch was my father's'. It is typical of most 17th century Lucases that we find crocks, pans, cows and breeches lovingly handed down from one generation to the next.

In 1597/8 John I had bought the Llanmorlais estate in Llanrhidian Parish. This property in Welsh Gower included the lower part of the Morlais valley on the north side of the peninsula, where the Morlais stream flows into the marshy creeks of the Burry estuary. The sides of the valley are cut down from the north Gower plateau through the coal measures, leaving seams of coal exposed or near the surface. It seems surprising for a yeoman farmer from Stouthall to launch out into an investment of this kind at so early a period, and we do not know whether John knew of the commercial possibilities of his purchase. But by the middle of the 17th century there was increasing interest in the coal deposits of the Morlais valley. During the 1650s Henry II, who had married his cousin Margaret heiress of Stouthall and granddaughter of John I, turned his attention to the coal seams at the Wern, a piece of land on the southern slopes of the valley. Here he 'set forth a coale workes by his tenant or agent and received land monies for the said coales wrought neere the midst of the said Wern'. Henry had some difficulty in establishing his right to the Wern part of which had been fenced off by a local farmer and cultivated. Henry took a firm line, and the farmer offered little resistance when Henry 'came to brake down the fences thereof; at which time the encroacher having sown turneeps thereon desired that he might quietly hold the same till he had had his turneeps, promising to pay a penny acknowledgement for the same at Michaelmas following'.

These Gower coal mines in the Morlais valley in the 17th century were quite small affairs, either drifts dug into the hillside or more usually bell pits. Each pit might be six to ten feet across and anything from six to twenty feet deep. They were widened or belled out at the bottom as far as safety allowed. The coal landed at the Wern was sold at the pit head and much of it was probably carted down the short distance to the Burry estuary where there was a flourishing coal export trade by sea. The coal was measured in 'weys', each of about fifty bags, and the miners were entitled to an allowance of four bags per wey. During the period from the 24th July to the 27th November 1686 the Wern produced 254 weys sold at a net profit of £38–3–0. By the year 1712 the Lucases seem to have lost interest in coal mining, and disposed of most of their mines on a long lease in return for royalties and — perhaps the best part of the bargain for Stouthall — 'three loads of firecoal weekly so long as there shall be coal on the land'. These coal mines were, so far as I can discover, the one and only business venture ever undertaken by the Lucases other than farming.

By the early years of the 18th century there were no Lucases left at Hills, and the Stouthall branch of the family were established as the Reynoldston village squires, and as farmers whose reputation as innovators extended beyond the confines of the Gower peninsula. Around the turn of the century they had been the first Gower farmers to experiment with the cultivation of red clover. This was an important step forward in the production of cattle feed. Henry Lucas III, described by Walter Davies writing on Welsh Agriculture many years later as 'one of the first agriculturists of his time' made a further innovation after a disastrous frost had destroyed his autumn sown clover crop in the year 1716. 'Not willing to forgo his clover crop for a whole year he made an experiment to sow it with barley in the Spring; it of course succeeded; his neighbours followed his example; and from that time to the present clover is generally sown with Spring crops, barley, oats, and sometimes with beans.'

Henry III was a farmer who looked well beyond his cows and his clover. He sent his eldest son John IV first to Balliol College Oxford where he took his degree and then to study law at the Middle Temple. Foreign travel was encouraged and Henry probably went abroad. His son John certainly did, and it became usual for Lucas young men to do the 'grand tour' of France, Spain and Italy. The oldest family possessions which have survived date from the time of Henry III; his 'basket bible' of 1736, and a fine glazed blue and white plate made at Talavera in Spain or possibly Savona in Italy around 1700. It has an attractive design with a charming and lively bird as its centrepiece. I like to think that it caught the eye of young Henry on his travels.

Henry III became High Sheriff of Glamorgan in 1744, a post in which he was followed by his son, grandson and great grandson. The High Sheriffs served for a year. They were appointed by the Crown and were responsible for law and order and the administration of justice within the County. Until the time of the Civil War the appointment was an important one and accounted a great honour, but from the Restoration onwards it declined in importance. By the mid 18th century it was little more than a ceremonial post and shunned by the grander gentry on account of the heavy fees and expenses involved. They used such influence as they possessed to avoid being 'drafted', and a newly appointed Sheriff might expect to receive letters of condolence from his friends more appropriate to a bereavement than to the award of a Royal Honour. Nonetheless the more substantial of the Gower squires took their turns with fortitude, and no doubt acquired some kudos among their neighbours in the peninsula, if not among the more sophisticated gentry of the Vale of Glamorgan.

In 1702 Henry III had married Jane Phillips of Cheriton whose mother was Katherine Seys descended from the Boverton family. This union with the Phillips was the first of a series of marriages which transformed the prospects and may have ultimately caused the dissolution of the Stouthall inheritance. For the previous three generations the Stouthall Lucases had married Hills cousins and before that they had usually married into other Gower farming families, Bakers, Sumllys, Batcocks, Groves, Bennetts and Bidders. Farming has always been very much a family affair and for one young farmer to marry the sister of another young farmer in the next parish was then, as indeed it is today, a sound basis on which to maintain the fortunes of the family business. But from 1700 onwards the family seems to have adopted a deliberate policy of marrying the eldest son of the house to an heiress, that is to say a young lady with no brothers and preferably no sisters either, so that she could be relied upon to bring her family land and fortune with her. The Phillips family came from Devon to Swansea about the time of Queen Elizabeth I. In or about 1657 Jane's grandfather Thomas Phillips purchased an estate at Cheriton, including the Great House, from the Cradocks who had lived there since medieval times. The Great House stood a little to the south of the bridge in Cheriton, on the opposite side of the road to the churchyard. It was a substantial house, probably built in about 1600 by Morgan Cradock, and comparable to Pitt and old Stouthall.

The eldest son of the marriage of Henry Lucas III and Jane Phillips was John the elder who made the second of the 'heiress' marriages. His bride was Hannah Nicholas (1717–65). The Nicholas family claimed descent from Roger Clarendon an illegitimate son of Edward the Black Prince. Their ancient family home was at Garthen opposite the village of Clydach in the Vale of Tawe. This situation on the lower slopes of Mynydd Drumau facing west across the quiet water meadows of the Tawe towards the high land of Blaen Gower must have been a place of peace and beauty before the industrial revolution came to the lower Swansea valley.

Hannah had five brothers and sisters but as she inherited the Garthen property they presumably died young. Hannah and John the elder were married at St. Mary's Church Swansea on the 18th April 1738. She was 20 and John was 34. She brought with her an entitlement on her parents' death to the mansion house at Garthen and some 400 acres of farmland with houses and cottages, all in the Parish of Llansamlet in the lower Swansea valley. It seems likely that she also brought to Stouthall a disastrous train of ill health, probably tuberculosis, which resulted in her death at the early age of 48. She and John had six children. When she died three of them had already died in infancy, and John was left with Henry the eldest son then aged 25, Hannah aged 16 and the youngest, John, a little boy of 6. The following year Hannah died, and the next year, despite a desperate search for health in a continental tour, Henry 'left his afflicted father at Pezenas October the 27th 1768 and was buried at Montag in Languedoc in France aged 28 years'. Only little John, John the Younger as he came to be known, survived to inherit Stouthall.

John the elder was a sober sort of a squire, unlike many of his contemporaries, and much concerned for the welfare of his tenants.

He would only permit his son to inherit the Stouthall estates on condition that all the tenants were allowed to keep their holdings undisturbed. The tenants' moral welfare was a more tricky problem. Inspired perhaps by John Bunyan, he decided that new names would help in this direction. Cefn-y-Garth, a farm on his wife's property in the lower Swansea valley, was renamed Prosperity. Gone were many of the old Gower names in Cheriton Parish, and the astonished tenants, Bevans, Howells and Hopkins, found their cottages and vegetable patches renamed Forecast, Prudence, Dexterity, Diligence and Industry. When John died his executors received a legacy of £10 'to be laid out in buying good books of piety for the use of my tenants and others who may want them'. Despite the good books of piety the new names did not catch on, and with the arrival of the 19th century the old ones, Cefn-y-Garth and rest, reappear.

So far I have said little about younger children who in early days often had to seek a livelihood outside Gower — the Church the Law and the Army were traditional — while their eldest brother inherited the family estates. Some of the problems of a younger son are seen in this letter from Edward Mansel of Henllys in Rhosili Parish to William Lucas serving in a dragoon regiment in Lisbon. William had a small farm at Newton next to Henllys but perhaps joined the army to try to solve his money problems.

> Sir,
> I am glad to hear by yours to your wife of ye ninthe of
> December last yt you are wel, and in the land of the living.
> Hear having been a current discours yt you were dead. It
> pleases me to finde that you are in the Brigadeer's favour,
> and the rest of your officers; you mention having writ to Sir
> Thomas Mansel (who is made a lord) and to Sr Peter King;
> if it be about any Preferment take this caution, that my
> Lord will have nothing to do with any Body that depends
> on Sr Peter, (and God be praised) Sr Peter nor no Whigg
> or Fanatique are in repute hear, times are altered. All your
> relations are wel only Mr Seys and his lady of Boverton are
> now ill.
> As to your own affairs I can only tel you that for the first
> year Sam: Jones had the management and delivered so
> much to your wife at very extravagant Rates, that none of
> my Lord Mansel's Arrears was payd, but now (having
> taken it out of Sam Jones' hands) the Arrears of my Lord's
> was left last Michaelmas almost payd of, and John Button
> delivered to your wife what was necessary, which is also
> payd, so that at Lady Day the small matter wch remains wil

be payd of, your wife have a better allowance, and other
creditors, as your uncle Portrey, Mr Hopkins etc; wil one
after another be payd of. I wil take care that the rents shal
as they become due be carefully applyed, to clear My Lord,
pay the creditors, and allow a good competency to your
wife.

   We have an accompt heer that my cozen and your good
friend Major Bennet is Basaly killed in Spain, if it be
possible enquire out the truth of it He was taken prisoner
at Brithuga. We are in expectation of a peace, if you have
any news let us have it, and the History of your life since I
saw you all heer remember them to you as does
   Dear Will,
      Your faithful friend
         E. Mansel

                    Henllys March ye 3d 1711/12

   This William Lucas was probably a great nephew of George
Lucas the younger of Hills. Edward Mansel lived at old Henllys
until in 1715 he sold his estate to his kinsman Sir Thomas First
Lord Mansel mentioned in the letter. Sir Peter King, later to
become Lord Chancellor of England, had married a daughter of
Richard Seys of Boverton, the Mr Seys referred to. King was a
Whig and Mansel was a high Tory, and at the date of the letter the
Tories were in power and dedicated to bringing the war of the
Spanish Succession to an end; hence Mansel's timely warning.
Uncle Portrey was the Reverend Richard Portrey then Rector of
Rhosili and a man of property, who was connected with the
Lucases by marriage.

   Another younger son Richard Lucas, Henry III's younger
brother, was the founder of a branch of the family which, not
having enough land to make a living, turned very successfully to
the Church and the learned professions. Richard owned a property
in Reynoldston Parish, Peartree later to be renamed Fairyhill. But
rather than stay in Gower and play second fiddle to Henry at
Stouthall, Richard obtained a post as steward (resident land agent)
to the Taliaris estate of the Gwynne family. Taliaris, an imposing
Jacobean mansion, is some five miles north of Llandilo. Built by
the Gwynnes in about 1635, the house is set on a hillside above the
Dulais river in a remote and beautiful landscape with wide views to
the south across the valley of the Tywi to a horizon bounded by the
high desolate ridges of the Black Mountain. In about 1718, while
at Taliaris, Richard married Barbara the daughter of a neighbouring squire Owen Bowen of Gurrey Manor. There will be more to

say of the Bowens later.

Richard Lucas and his wife kept their Gower home and in due course retired to spend the rest of their days at Peartree. Their eldest son John, a clergyman, also retired there. Another son, Henry Lloyd Lucas, qualified as a surgeon at a time when the surgeons, casting off their traditional association with the barbers, had founded their own College and were beginning to rise in the social and professional scale. This Henry lived at Penmaes in

Mrs Anne Williams, daughter of Richard Lucas of Peartree, c. 1760

Carmarthenshire and was the first of a line of Lucas medical men who achieved distinguished careers in and around Carmarthen, Brecon and Crickhowell. They were a scholarly family, and one of Henry's great grandsons, Charles (1853–1931), acquired fame and a knighthood as historian of the British Empire. Sir Charles was proud of his Gower descent and to the traditional family coat of arms, a fesse or sword belt between six annulets, he added a golden palm tree on a blue background. Students of Kipling may ask why he omitted the pine.

Another of Richard Lucas's children, Anne, married the Reverend John Williams in 1760. Williams was the Rector of Cheriton, a Parish next to Reynoldston. The Parsonage was in disrepair so the Rector and his wife rented the Great House which, as we have seen, now belonged to Mrs Williams's Stouthall cousins. The old Parsonage or Glebe house caused the Williams a lot of bother. For one thing it was haunted. According to the Gower historian The Reverend J. D. Davies, who was himself Rector of Cheriton in the 19th century:

> The story goes that this ghost was the spirit of a lady who once farmed the glebe land and used to dispose of the produce of the dairy, such as butter milk and cheese, to the inhabitants of the place; but not giving just weight, her spirit could not rest, and after death returned to haunt the house, terrifying the inmates with doleful cries of 'Weight and Measure' 'Weight and Measure' many times repeated, while dreadful noises, as of heavy things falling down, and a quick shrill rattling of all the jugs on the dresser, with a confused rushing to and fro of something that could not be seen, became at last so unbearable that Mr. Williams was called in to bind the spirit — 'and he' as my informant related, 'was an Oxford scholar, you know'. [This is not quite correct for the Rector was in fact a Fellow of Kings College Cambridge.] In this he fortunately succeeded, but it was as much as he could do, and hard work he had of it, being shut up for two days and two nights in the blue chamber, the people of the house hearing him cracking his whip and talking Latin the whole time. It is also said that he got the mastery only by one word, and that the spirit was bound to make ropes of sand on Llanmadoc burrows, and to remain there 'till she done it'.

It does rather look as though the spirit tried to take her revenge on the parson; as in 1776 one George Bevan brought a vexatious action at law against the Rector on the grounds of his non-residence at the Glebe house. This might have resulted in Williams losing his benefice. The best legal advice was taken from an eminent Counsel, Lloyd Kenyon, later to become Lord Chief Justice, who expressed the view that the complaint was well founded according to a strict interpretation of the law; although Williams would have the strong sympathy of the Court and Jury, living as he did within one hundred yards of the Church, and furthermore 'He keeps no curate, he does the whole duty of the parish, is truly hospitable and charitable, he is beloved and respected by all his parishioners'. We do not know the result of the case; probably it never came to trial, and Williams was still Rector of Cheriton when he died at the Great House in 1787.

2

1751–78
The Welsh Squires —
The Murder at Glanareth

The next heiress to marry into the Lucas family, Catherine Powell, who was to become the wife of John Lucas the younger of Stouthall, came from a background that can hardly be described as either sober or industrious. Hitherto the family inheritance was from a long line of worthy and moderately cultured squires and farmers from Gower and the Vale of Glamorgan. The blood which Catherine brought to the family was from a very different source. Indeed this may have been true in a literal sense as the remote part of Wales, the Black Mountain of Carmarthenshire, where the Powells had their property has been shown to have an exceptionally high frequency of blood group B among its inhabitants. This comparatively rare blood group among West European people may, it has been suggested, represent the survival in this part of Wales of very early human stocks possibly dating back even as far as the Upper Palaeolithic period.

But whatever their remote ancestry may have been, this branch of the Powells seems to have been rough and unruly. Catherine's father was William Powell, son of Walter Powell of Glantowe, and her mother was Catherine, daughter of John Bowen whose sister Barbara had married Richard Lucas of Peartree. Walter Powell was High Sheriff of Carmarthenshire in 1752 in which year, according to a note in the Lloyd family records, his son William was tried, and acquitted, of the murder of a servant girl at Glantowe whom his father had taken as mistress. Whatever the truth of this story Walter does not seem to have borne a grudge against his son as a few years later he made a will leaving all his very substantial property to William. This consisted of some 3500 acres, divided into about 60 farms, cottages and smallholdings, spread in a great arc along the western borders of Blaen Gower and the western and northern slopes of the Black Mountain. The holdings ranged from lowland farms in the Llandeilo Talybont area of mainland Gower to the hill farms around Bettws, Llandebie, Carreg Cennan, Llandeilo fawr and Llangadog; and at Llandeusant, perched above the ravine where the Afon Sawdde brawls and tumbles down the northern side of the Black Mountain from the dark waters of Llyn y fan fach. It is surprising to find that the heir to all this property, who married Catherine Bowen in March 1758, could neither read nor write.

The Bowens of Gurrey Manor were an old Welsh family who traced their descent back to Sir Elidir Ddu, a Knight of the Holy Sepulchre who lived at Gurrey and made his pilgrimage to Jerusalem early in the 14th century. They were, as we have seen, already connected with the Lucases by marriage. Richard Lucas's brother-in-law John Bowen, Catherine's father, had married Anne Lloyd heiress of Llawryllan, and it is through her that the Lucases can claim kinship with other notable Welsh families tracing their line back not only to King Edward I of England but through the mists of antiquity to Rhodri Mawr the last of the princes who ruled the whole of Wales and who was killed by the Saxons in the ninth century. Anne Lloyd's mother was Mary Johnes of Abermaes. Some of the Lloyds and the Johnes of the 18th century and earlier were a rough lot. The most notorious of the Lloyds lived at Maes y felin (Millfield) and Peterwell near Lampeter. The Maes y felin branch of the family had been comprehensively cursed by the famous Vicar Pritchard of Llandovery in the 17th century, but the curse had little effect on them and by the mid 18th century Lucius Lloyd had established a reputation for drinking dicing and whoring which awed his contemporaries even in those rumbustious times. Even worse was Herbert Lloyd of Peterwell a Justice of the Peace whose name became a byword for villainy and corruption. He it was who waged the famous vendetta against his neighbour Shon Phillips a simple farmer whose only offence was to own a property in the middle of the Peterwell estate which he steadfastly refused to sell to Herbert Lloyd who coveted it. Eventually Lloyd put about the story that a black ram had been stolen from his flocks. A few nights later, when Phillips and his wife were asleep in their house, Lloyd had the ram dropped down their chimney. The bailiff and constable who had been summoned in readiness broke into the house, discovered the ram in the parlour, and thereupon arrested Phillips and put him in gaol. Lloyd then offered not to prosecute if Phillips would convey the land to him, but Phillips still refused. Herbert Lloyd then sent him for trial for sheep stealing, for which he was convicted and hanged. With Shon Phillips out of the way a forged title deed gave Lloyd what he wanted.

By no means all of Catherine Bowen's kinsfolk were disreputable. Her niece married John Johnes of Dolaucothi whose sister Jane married a cousin Thomas Johnes of Hafod (1748–1816). Thomas was a scholar, a man of most unusual quality. He translated Froissart's Chronicles and assembled a famous library at Hafod in the wilds of Cardiganshire. He was a philanthropist who expended vast sums on estate management for the benefit of his poverty stricken tenants. The tragic story of Thomas and Jane Johnes and their daughter Mariamne has been told by Elisabeth Inglis-Jones in her book *Peacocks in Paradise*. Despite some aberrations, Anne Lloyd's family were important and influential landowners and her marriage to John Bowen must have been looked on favourably by the Bowens; Richard Lucas seems to have been proud of it since he gave the names Henry Lloyd to his son who was born at about the same time as his brother-in-law contracted this marriage

Catherine, daughter of John Bowen of Gurrey and wife of William Powell
From a portrait attributed to Sir Thomas Lawrence

Such was the background of Catherine Bowen the future mother-in-law of John Lucas the younger of Stouthall. Although her disastrous marriage to William Powell and the sensational murder with which it ended received wide publicity at the time there are several questions which are unlikely ever to be answered. One is why John Bowen allowed his daughter to marry a young man with such an unsatisfactory background as William Powell; for this was no runaway match but an arranged affair with Marriage Articles signed before the ceremony. Was Catherine headstrong, or was her father unable to resist the lure of those 3500 acres? It was usual among gentry families in the 18th century for the property rights of the bride and groom and their future children to be regulated by a Marriage Settlement which was often the subject of hard bargaining conducted between the family lawyers. Once the terms were agreed the Marriage Articles would be drawn up and signed before the wedding. The husband would usually 'settle' his landed property, or part of it, and the wife would settle hers, if she had any, or bring in capital in some form. The object would be to keep the land in the family for the benefit of future generations so far as the law allowed, to safeguard the wife's property and prevent the husband from getting control of it, and generally to protect the family fortunes from the worst effects of extravagance and folly. An essential feature was the appointment of trustees representing each side of the family. Once the articles or contract had been signed the marriage could go forward and the legal transfer of the property, known as the Settlement, would follow at a later date.

In the case of William Powell and Catherine Bowen the Marriage Articles contained some very unusual features. The sole trustee was to be the bride's father John Bowen, and the bridegroom agreed to hand over not only his prospective interest in the 3500 acres under his father's will — his father was still alive — but also the whole of his personal property which would include his furniture and effects and the very clothes he stood up in, and all his ready money, if he had any, to his future father-in-law. In return the Bowens put nothing into the settlement but gave William an almost derisory present of £100 in cash to spend as he wished. One can only guess at possible reasons why William accepted these terms. Perhaps Catherine was compromised and the marriage was forced on the young people by the social conventions of the day, or William may have got himself into a financial scrape. His own account of the matter, given 11 years later, was that the Marriage Articles were 'obtained from him by fraud imposition and surprise; that he was illiterate and could neither read nor write and that the same was not explained or read over to him by any person before the execution and that in case the same had been read over and explained to him he would not have executed the same'. Whatever the truth of the matter William steadfastly refused to implement the agreement or hand over any of the land or other property, and nothing more had been done when John Bowen died. For about 11 years William and Catherine lived together, mostly at Glanareth a house which belonged to the Powell family and which may have been built or rebuilt in 1762. This house was in or near the little hamlet of Pontprenareth, where the Areth stream flows down a narrow wooded valley from the foothills of the Black Mountain to join the Tywi river. There were two children of the marriage, Catherine born in 1761 and Anne born a year or two later.

We do not know much about the events which led to the break up of the marriage, but it appears that Mrs Powell had formed what was known in those days as a 'criminal connection' with one William Williams, known to his friends as Billy Williams, a married man who kept a draper's or haberdasher's shop in Llandovery; and that in August 1768 or 1769 she went off with Williams who took her, and her two little girls who had been in boarding school, to London. Legal proceedings followed. Powell applied unsuccessfully for custody of the children, and on 4th March 1769 a John Williams, thought to be Billy's brother, filed a bill in Chancery on behalf of the children with the object of forcing Powell to give effect to the Marriage Articles and transfer the property, which by now he had inherited from his father, to the Bowen family as trustees. Powell countered by making a will a few weeks later in which he left all his property to the two children, cut his wife out altogether, and appointed as his executors two well-known Swansea solicitors, his cousin the redoubtable Gabriel Powell the hard and unpopular agent for the Duke of Beaufort, and one Illtyd Thomas. On the 28th December 1769 he filed an answer to the Chancery suit alleging, as we have seen, that the marriage settlement was obtained by fraud, but offering to give his wife an annuity of £250. But by the time this offer was filed on the books of the Court of Chancery, Billy Williams was back in Llandovery planning Powell's murder.

Williams, an utterly ruthless villain, must have had an extraordinary power over women. Not only had he been able to persuade Mrs Powell to associate with him in the first place, but in pursuit of his design he had twice tried to make away with his own wife, if her story is to be believed, presumably to free himself to marry Mrs Powell. Yet Mrs Williams kept this to herself until many years afterwards. It seems remarkable that the crime which Williams was now planning, Powell's murder, did not come to the ears of the local magistrates, since it involved recruiting a gang of ruffians in Llandovery over a period of about a fortnight during what seems to have been a prolonged drinking spree in a public house, the New Bear. This is the inn which later came to be known as the Old Bear, and stood where 13 Market Square stands today on the opposite side of the square to the present Bear Inn. The principal members of Billy Williams' gang were William Spiggott a barber and publican; his son John Spiggott a servant; William Morris a saddler; William Thomas known as 'Blink' a glover; David Morgan known as 'Lacy' a tinker, and his apprentice Walter Evan; also William Walter Evan, Charles Morgan and his son William, and David Llewellin. The last four were farmers or smallholders. The apprentice Walter Evan, called Wat the tinker, turned King's evidence in the subsequent trial and it is mainly on him that we must rely for an account of the events which led up to the murder. The first attempt to kill Powell was abortive. Williams sent Wat the tinker and David Llewellin to murder him on his way to Swansea, but the assassins got no further than Llangadog where they became hopelessly drunk and lost their quarry. Powell returned from Swansea during the first few days of January, and on the night of the 7th Billy Williams assembled his gang at the house of Charles Morgan which was about a mile from Glanareth. The following evening at dusk they set out for Glanareth. By way of disguise they all blacked their faces and some of the party put on waggoners' frocks. Billy Williams carried a sword and the others a collection of pistols guns swords and tucks. David Morgan and Wat exchanged coats, and Charles Morgan put a handkerchief on his head to hide his red hair. It began to snow as the party made their way across the fields in the gathering darkness. As well as their weapons they carried a large bottle of rum from which they fortified themselves from time to time.

In the parlour at Glanareth, lit by a single candle on the mantel shelf, sat Powell dressed in a blue coat white waistcoat and black breeches. With him was a nephew and two other men. In the kitchen was Margaret Jones the maid servant, a young girl called

Sarah, a Mr Williams who was Powell's clerk and letter writer, and two of the workmen on the estate. There came a sharp knocking on the door, Sarah was sent to open it, and the gang rushed in. Wat the tinker ran to the kitchen door shouting out 'Stand back by God!' and brandishing a sword. John Williams the clerk seized a shovel and attacked the tinker. Another of the gang fired a pistol and at this point John Morgan, one of Powell's workmen, took the shovel and succeeded in driving his assailants out of the kitchen. Meanwhile Billy Williams and David Llewellin and some others burst into the parlour. Powell ran into a corner and his companions made their escape. Powell managed to fling Williams to the ground but he was quickly overpowered, savagely hacked and stabbed with sword thrusts, and left dying behind the parlour door. Within a couple of minutes the gang had departed and the house fell silent except for the gasps of the dying man and the terrified sobbing of Margaret and Sarah. A broken sword and William Spiggott's hat and his black wig lay on the floor of the parlour among the pools of blood.

The gang returned across the snow covered fields to Charles Morgan's house. At some stage they fell to quarrelling. Billy Williams who had promised them a hundred guineas each for their night's work gave no more than a single guinea to any of them, and soon set off alone on horseback leaving the rest of the party to fend for themselves. Meanwhile at Glanareth the alarm had been raised and at dawn next morning two of the local gentry took charge of the situation. The footprints and bloodstains in the snow were followed to Charles Morgan's house and careful measurements were taken of the print of a shoe with five nails and other prints of a fashionable style of boot 'too small and handsome for a Welsh farmer'. At the coroner's inquest Charles Morgan was ordered to pull off his shoe and it was found to correspond exactly with the mark in the snow, the dimensions of which had been carefully recorded. Evidence was given of the similarity of the fashionable boot print to a pair belonging to Billy Williams about which Williams had boasted in Llandovery that he had had them made in London off the same last as a pair made for the King of Denmark. It seems that the members of the gang were fairly well known around Llandovery, and at least one of them had been recognised in the kitchen at Glanareth, despite the blackened faces and waggoners' frocks. All with the exception of Williams were rounded up within a few days and put in gaol. Williams's mare was found near Newtown in Radnorshire but of the chief criminal himself there was no trace.

In March 1770 the prisoners were transferred from Carmarthen gaol to Hereford for trial, the operation being supervised by the High Sheriffs for the two Counties. The trial took place at the Hereford Assizes which opened on the 27th March, before Mr Justice Yates. The prisoners were represented by Counsel, and the trial, several reports of which were published and widely circulated, seems to have been very fairly conducted. The prisoners spoke only Welsh and the trial was carried on with the assistance of an interpreter. There seems to have been some prejudice against this man, as it is said that as he was on his way home after the trial a man 'disguised in an asses skin' jumped over a hedge and fired a gun at him. John Spiggott, William Thomas and Charles Morgan's son were acquitted. William Spiggott, William Morris, David Morgan, William Walter Evan, Charles Morgan and David Llewellin were convicted and on the 30th March they were hanged. Wat the tinker gave evidence for the Crown, but it did him little good as shortly afterwards he was hanged for his part in another crime. The bodies of Spiggott and Evan were hung in chains on Hardwick Common near Hay on Wye, and the remains of the other four murderers were handed over to the surgeons for dissection. Their victim William Powell had been buried in the chancel of Llangadog Church.

To what extent were Mrs Powell and her family implicated in this sordid crime? There is no direct evidence against Mrs Powell apart from statements allegedly made by Billy Williams who showed a large piece of gold to the conspirators which, he said, had come from Mrs Powell, adding that she would not prosecute them for killing her husband. On the other hand there was fairly strong suspicion against her brother Captain Marmaduke Bowen who lived at Cil-y-Cwm near Llandovery. Wat the tinker's story was that he and David Morgan and another man had been sent by Williams to Captain Bowen's house at Cil-y-Cwm on the Saturday before the murder to get them away from the notice of the people in Llandovery; that Captain Bowen had invited them in, and 'when I told him very plain we were to kill Mr Powell, he clapped me on the back and said if I would do that I should never want and that there should never be any prosecution against me for it'. The Captain then, according to the tinker, said that he could not accommodate them but he gave them a note to the innkeeper in Cil-y-Cwm with instructions that they should be given a crown's worth of meat and drink; and later Captain Bowen joined the men at the Inn, spent a further two shillings on them, and they all 'talked strangely' about Mr Powell. Such evidence is hardly worth much, but it seems that there must have been more to it since on April 13th Captain Bowen was arrested in London 'at the Cock eating house behind the Royal Exchange' and charged in connection with the murder at Hereford Summer Assizes along with his son Lewis Lloyd Bowen and Billy's brother John Williams. The case against the latter two was presumably that they had been concerned in aiding the escape of Billy Williams. The case was eventually tried before Mr Justice Ashurst at the Lent Assizes in 1771. The prosecution evidence was unconvincing. Several gentlemen gave evidence of Captain Bowen's irreproachable character and the jury was only out for five minutes before acquitting all three prisoners.

In fact Mrs Powell and her friends had not been idle since the murder. According to one contemporary account, on the very night of the murder 'one of the villains was dispatched by Williams to inform Mr Powell's brother what was done, and ordering him to come and take possession of the estates; but Mr Powell having made a will and appointed guardians over his children the scheme was defeated'. This does not make sense as Williams would hardly have wanted the Powell family to come in at this juncture. The reference to a brother is probably meant for Williams's own brother John who was at this time the official 'next friend' suing on behalf of the Powell children in the Chancery action. What happened was that Gabriel Powell and Illtyd Thomas, the executors and guardians appointed by Powell in his will, immediately took over the dead man's property. John Williams countered by filing a 'Bill of Revivor' in Chancery in the names of the two children, claiming that Powell had no power to deal with the property in his will and that the legal ownership should pass in accordance with the Marriage Articles, i.e. to the family of Mrs Powell. When the trial of the murderers came on at Hereford both Mrs Powell and her husband's executors were there, and they took the opportunity to engage in what was no doubt some hard bargaining. The result was an agreement whereby the Chancery proceedings were dropped, Mrs Powell renounced her claims to the estate of her murdered husband in return for a life annuity of £300, and Gabriel Powell and Illtyd Thomas were confirmed as trustees of the Powell estates on behalf of the two children Catherine and Anne. The agreement was dated 11th April 1770. Nowadays when so much is said about the law's delay it is interesting to reflect that within three months of the date of the murder all but one of the assassins had been captured, tried and hanged, a complicated Chancery action had been settled, and the devolution of the murdered man's estates had been arranged to everyone's apparent satisfaction.

Anne Powell, daughter of William Powell of Glanareth. From a miniature c. 1785.

In 1778 the elder daughter Catherine, now aged 16 or 17, married John Lucas the younger of Stouthall. In or about 1785 Mrs Powell remarried. Her new husband was Cyprian Rondeau Bunce of Canterbury, a gentleman who seems to have been situated at a comfortable distance from Llandovery. Catherine's younger sister Anne died unmarried and intestate in April 1787, and those 3500 acres became effectively part of the Stouthall estate. In the Lucas and Lloyd families the story of the Powell murder was either hushed up or bowdlerised so as to remove all suggestion of marital infidelity or involvement by Mrs Powell or her family. Indeed a story put out by the Lloyd family went so far as to have the murder take place after Mrs Powell's death. In the 19th century the children at Stouthall were told that 'an ancestor had been shot by Fenians while drinking his after dinner port with the light on and the curtains not drawn.'

What happened to Billy Williams? His fate is surrounded by rumour and mystery. All stories have him taking refuge in France. According to one account he was captured by the British navy while serving as a common seaman in a French privateer, but escaped from a prison camp at Alton and once more disappeared into obscurity. Another story was that he became a fisherman in northern France and was drowned 'at an advanced age'. Yet another tale was that he kept a school at St Omer, and was drowned while bathing with his pupils. There were reports that his papers were found at Boulogne, and one person who remembered as a boy meeting his widow at Llandovery wrote: 'I saw a copy book of his for the year after the murder, and there was a spot of blood on the anniversary of the fatal day, and a note to this effect: "My finger bled today — how singular!" '

Mrs Catherine Powell, c. 1785, widow of William Powell.

3

1779–1830
The Gower Gentry — The New Stouthall

Catherine, wife of John Lucas the younger, c. 1785

When John Lucas the younger married Catherine Powell in 1778 they went to live at Lincombe House in Bath. Their affairs were regulated by comprehensive Marriage Articles dated 24th December 1777. This was a wide ranging and fair document, quite unlike that unhappy contract which had compounded the disaster which had befallen Catherine's parents. John and Catherine's settlement was immensely long, some 12 000 words taking five 'skins' of closely written parchment, each skin measuring 30 inches by 24 inches. Six copies of this formidable document were prepared so that each of the trustees should have a copy. In the days of instant reproduction and word processing one is apt to forget the laborious industry of the old lawyers' clerks perched on their high stools with the tools of their trade, the skins and the sealing wax, the bottles of pounce and ink powder, and the quill pens, drafting and copying all through the daylight hours of their working lives.

The Powell and Lucas estates were entailed in the manner known as 'tail male'. This meant that everything went to the eldest son on the father's death, and if there were no male heirs of this son then the male heirs of his younger brother would take the property in priority to the daughters.

Catherine was to receive a personal allowance or 'pin money' of £50 per year (to be increased to £100 after her mother's death) 'for her own sole and separate use and benefit for her cloaths and other her occasions as she shall think fit without the controul and intermeddling of John Lucas the younger her intended husband'.

A Stouthall Lucas, said to be Hannah, wife of John Lucas the elder

In about 1784 the Rev John Lucas left Peartree and went to live in Cheriton, presumably to join his sister Mrs Anne Williams, and John and Catherine were quick to take the opportunity of returning to Gower. By 1785 they were living at Peartree which they renamed Fairyhill. Catherine's sister Anne died in April 1787 and on 10th September of that year John Lucas the elder died at Stouthall.

We now come to the rebuilding of Stouthall. The house which John and Catherine built still stands, square set and plain; perhaps too plain one may feel at a first sight of the house through the tracery of the beech trees along the main road to Porteynon. From this aspect the house with its gaunt outline and tall windows appears out of sympathy with its surroundings. Viewed from Reynoldston the effect is different. The pale façade beneath the low-pitched slate roof against a dark background of trees has a comfortably dignified air and makes a pleasing focal point in the landscape. One is too far away for the eye to be distracted by the modern offices clapped on either side of the main entrance, yet near enough to distinguish the splashes of red from the rhododendrons, and to hear the distant cawing of the rooks. This was the elegant residence on which John and Catherine had set their hearts and upon which they lavished 'all those softer beauties which taste could dictate'.

The date 1754 sometimes given for the building of the present house is certainly wrong. It comes from a suspect source and is easily disproved. John Williams's map of Reynoldston was published in 1784 and shows not the new house but the old Stouthall as described in an earlier chapter. The architect was the well-known Swansea man William Jernagen who was born in 1750, and who was responsible for a number of local buildings, including the Mumbles Lighthouse, between 1790 and 1810. The fact that Jernagen was staying at old Stouthall only a few months after John Lucas the elder's death suggests that one of the first things to which John the younger turned his attention after entering on his inheritance was the rebuilding of the mansion house. John and Catherine continued living at Fairyhill until at least May 1791. By May 1793 they were at Stouthall.

So it seems likely that Stouthall was completed between 1791 and 1793. The house is built in the Palladian style so popular in the 18th century and shows the strong influence of the Adams brothers, both in design of the building and the interior decoration. The main entrance and the portico form the central feature in the north façade. The hall rises through two floors and is surrounded by a gallery on three sides giving access to the principal bedrooms. This gallery is decorated with columns and reached by a fine stairway. The cornice mouldings of the hall have a design of animals' skulls. The large west drawing room, and the dining room decorated with columns, moulded cornices, and low-relief ceiling mouldings, are separated by the library, a most unusual and beautiful room of elliptical shape and fine decorative treatment. Opposite the Adam-style fireplace in this room is the well-known secret door in the library shelves giving access to the drawing room and providing, no doubt, a most convenient bolt hole for any member of the family trapped in the drawing room by the arrival of unexpected guests in the front hall. The southern end of the library projects to form a bow window in the southern façade of the house. The east wing of the building contained a set of rooms used at one time as a billiard room, gun room and smoking room, also the kitchen, servants' hall and housekeeper's room. This wing was at a lower level, by about five feet, than the

John Lucas the younger, c. 1775

Catherine, wife of John Lucas the younger, by W. Shuter 1788.

ground floor of the main building. The floor of the billiard room and gun room was subsequently raised to conform with the rest. Jernagen, like Thomas Ivory in Suffolk and Thomas Hopper who designed Margam and Llanover, was at one time a clerk of works and pupil of John Johnson who set him up in business.

When John the younger inherited Stouthall he took over what was basically a farmer's house set in traditional farmland, for although his father had been a substantial landowner he did not enjoy around Stouthall anything resembling the park bequeathed to posterity by his son. The land between Stouthall and Reynold-ston village was a jumble of small enclosed fields in varying ownership, part meadow part arable, interspersed with the undivided strip cultivations dating back to Norman times.

Young John set about acquiring these fields and strips of land between the house and the village. He planted trees and laid out a park of some 40 acres. He built stables and other outbuildings, including an elaborate grotto in the romantic style, excavated an ice-house, and probably established the walled garden. John also indulged in what Mr Davies the Rector of Reynoldston used to describe as 'Mr Lucas's whims'. He erected a 'prehistoric' stone circle in a field on the left of the road as you enter the village from the south, and buried a favourite horse under a burial mound in a field on the opposite side of the road, surmounting it by a sculptured pillar stone which he had probably found lying on his property. This pillar stone bears Celtic carving of great antiquity, dating probably from the ninth century, and may be the earliest Christian monument to be found in Gower. It was moved into Reynoldston Church in 1977 to avoid the slow weathering and flaking of the surface.

The grotto seems to have been a particular source of pride to the young squire. The story of its construction is told in Lewis's *Topographical Dictionary of Wales* published in the 1830s:

> In the same grounds there is one of the most extensive caverns in the Kingdom (sic) accidentally discovered by the late Mr Lucas, who, perceiving a small aperture in the limestone rock, containing a very strong clay, proceeded to clear it out; and finding the cavity expand inwards, he fully explored the interior, by removing several thousand tons of clay, and occasionally blasting the rock. The bottom of the cavern is a plain surface, about forty feet below the level of the ground, and the roof which is finely arched varies from ten to thirty six feet in height; it is capable of containing two thousand persons, and is entered in one part by a long flight of steps, rudely formed, and in another by a gradual descent; the interior, which has an imposing grandeur of appearance, is tolerably lighted by some natural openings in the incumbent strata.

Lewis omits to mention that John filled the holes in the roof of the cave with coloured glass, which he must have greatly valued as he makes a special note about it in his own handwriting at the end of his will. Lewis's description of the size of the cave sounds rather exaggerated, but it is difficult to be sure as the cave is now very much filled up with rubbish. The story that it is the start of a secret passage leading to Porteynon is (alas!) an invention. The cave does however connect with a system of underground water courses and is apt to fill suddenly with water in a mysterious way.

There can be little doubt that the building of this fine mansion and the conversion of a farm into a gentleman's country residence marked a fundamental change in the relationship of Stouthall with the rest of the Lucas estates in Gower. Hitherto Stouthall had been the centre of farming life in Reynoldston and beyond. From now on the family at Stouthall were landlords rather than farmers and probably took more from the land than they contributed. It is unlikely that this change could have taken place without the capital provided by the Powell properties. By 1796 the family finances were tangled. There were mortgage debts of £9800 secured on the Lucas and Powell estates; no doubt much of this money had been borrowed to pay for the building. The trouble was that there was no legal way of unscrambling Catherine's settled share of the Powell property from the half share which she had inherited from her sister Anne and this double ownership caused insoluble problems for her legal advisers; so much so that in 1796 a special private Act of Parliament was passed to resolve the matter. For the purpose of this Act all the Powell properties were valued. More than half the land, some 2200 acres valued at £16 558, was brought into the Stouthall settled estate. The remaining 1325 acres valued at £13 090 were allocated to Catherine as her absolute property. Her mother's annuity was charged equally between the two shares, and the burden of the family mortgage debt was also divided between them.

John the younger and Catherine had seven children. There were three boys, John Nicholas, George, and Henry; and four girls, Mary Catherine who died under 21, Caroline, Harriet and Matilda. Henry who was born in 1797 was the youngest of the family. The eldest son was John Nicholas, born in about 1784. George's life ended in tragedy. On 9th December 1799 the Rev John Collins Rector of Oxwich recorded in his diary: 'Poor Master G. Lucas killed by gun gone off'; and on the following day: 'Messrs Green Lucases and Edwards expected to dine with us on venison. Disappointed by melancholy event at Stouthall.' *The Gentleman's Magazine* for 1799 records for the 16th December: 'This day, as the two sons of J. Lucas Esq of Stouthall were preparing for a shooting party, the elder (sic) returning into his bedroom with a gun in his hand by some accident it went off and killed him on the spot.' At the time John was aged about 15 and George 13 or 14. George's name does not appear in the family pedigree, and the name never recurs in the family. Legend grew around the memory of George Lucas; he was said to have been handsome and charming, and to have been shot in a quarrel about a girl; and to this day children at Stouthall grow wide-eyed at the stories of the bloodstains still to be seen on the bedroom floor. But why was

George omitted from the pedigree, and why was the page recording his death cut out from the Stouthall copy of *The Gentleman's Magazine?*

The few gentry families in west Gower in the late 18th and early 19th centuries led an isolated social life and were thrown mostly on each other's resources. Dining out was the standard social event with occasional visits to Swansea to go to the play or the races, and perhaps once a year a visit to London or Bath. Dinner was at about 4.00 pm and the guests would remain to drink tea and play cards. On the more convivial occasions the guests would be given beds for the night and return to their homes the following morning. The principal families in the Stouthall social round were the Williams from Cheriton, the Edwards of Reynoldston, Collins of Oxwich, the Greens and later the Cowells from Fairyhill, and the Talbots of Penrice Castle. The Williams were, as we have seen, Lucas relations. The Rev James Edwards was Rector of Reynoldston from 1796 to 1834. In 1800, on the occasion of his forthcoming marriage to a Miss Sarah Lay, he leased from the Stouthall estate a property in Reynoldston then known as Shepherd's Lodge. This he either rebuilt or enlarged and renamed Brynfield. The Rev John Collins was Rector of Oxwich from 1772 to 1813. He married Ann, daughter of Robert Wells the Rector of Ilston, and they had ten children. Collins's diaries and correspondence are the source of much of our knowledge of everyday life among the Gower gentry of this period. Thomas Mansel Talbot was the son of the Rev Thomas Talbot of Lacock Abbey in Wiltshire from whom he inherited the Penrice and Margam estates. After a grand tour in Europe during which he amassed a quantity of antiques and paintings T. M. Talbot chose Penrice as his home and during the 1770s he built the present mansion house known as Penrice Castle. By way of a gatehouse on the main road he erected the sham ruin or folly now generally called The Towers. He became the friend and patron of John Collins for whom he built the new Oxwich Rectory to replace the old rectory washed away by the sea in the late 18th century.

In the summer months these few families not only dined at each other's houses, but organised outings and picnics; there was a visit to the Grotto at Stouthall, to the 'cavern', presumably the Culver Hole, at Porteynon, and excursions to the Worm's Head. In the spring of 1802 Miss Porter the governess at Penrice wrote in her journal: 'The party set out to see Worm's Head — returned at 7. Dear Lady Mary obliged to go to bed directly wet to the skin . . .

they went in open carriages but dined under a tent.' In the winter there were shooting parties and T. M. Talbot had a pack of hounds at Penrice. There was at this time a hunt known as the Worm's Head Hunt in which the huntsmen wore a uniform with silver buttons engraved with the words *Worms Head Hunt* and showing a rocky headland with a three masted square rigged ship. There is a tradition that this was an otter hunt.

What kind of a person was John Lucas the younger ? In trying to assess his character we see him mainly through the eyes of the Talbot and Collins families. Collins was a man of choleric disposition quick to take offence; and John Lucas had some reason to be jealous of the Talbots. Since Tudor times the occupants of Penrice — first the Bennetts then a junior branch of the Mansels and latterly Hancorn the surgeon — had been intimates of the Stouthall family and of a similar social status. The advent of the newcomer Thomas Mansel Talbot with his wealth and energy, his fine new mansion and his grandiose plans for the embellishment of his estate, entirely changed the relationship between Penrice and Stouthall. The squire of Stouthall had to play second fiddle to his dominating neighbour, and if John reacted by becoming prickly it is hardly surprising.

T. M. Talbot was apt to take a hard line with his Gower neighbours. There was trouble over the shooting rights. Old Mr Hancorn, now living at Pitt as a tenant of the Penrice estate, had walked over the estate with a gun for as long as he could remember, and saw no reason to change his habits. Talbot reacted by writing to Collins requesting him to intimate to Hancorn 'that if he runs riot I am determined to take every advantage the law allows me and at all events I shall insist on his leaving Pitt should he ever after carry a gun to the south of Keven Bryn'. On 31st January 1787 the Rev John Williams Rector of Cheriton died. He had, in addition to Cheriton, the living of Nicholaston worth £40 per year which was in the gift of the Manor of Penrice. The following day Collins wrote to Talbot who was away from home telling him of Williams's death and in the same letter asking for Nicholaston and giving as his reason 'the probability of an increase in my family' a circumstance in which 'the £40 per annum would be thought an happy addition to my income'. Another equally precipitate applicant was stout old parson Watkyn Knight, who already had the livings of Llanmadoc and Reynoldston. As Collins already had Oxwich and Llwchwr it might be thought that they started equal, but Knight was tactless enough to 'remind' Talbot that Nicholaston had been consolidated with Reynoldston — which was not strictly true as although this had been mooted it had never been carried through — and that Talbot had no right to consider anyone else for the job. Collins got the preferment, and Knight received a blistering letter from Talbot penned, as Talbot put it, 'in such a manner as I hope will ever prevent my seeing him again at Penrice or elsewhere'.

But when all allowances are made there can be little doubt that John was not an easy man to get on with. His neighbours did not know quite how to take him and his whims. There was friction over the new Gower postal service which had been set up by the efforts of the local gentry in 1799, with a post office in Reynoldston. In this year the letters were brought out to Reynoldston from Swansea 'by a little girl', and it was not only letters which the postwoman would deliver and collect from each house. In 1805 Collins recorded: 'Sent my brother (in Swansea) a basket of plants and seeds by postwoman. To the Postwoman carriage of basket to my brother 9d'. In the same year Joseph Green the London business man who had rented Fairyhill after the Lucases moved to Stouthall wrote to Collins: 'I am surprised Mr Lucas should undertake to regulate the Swansea Post without the concurrence of his neighbours who, I recollect, used to contribute to it much more largely than he did — my opinion is the less it is interfered with the better, or it may perhaps be wholly stopt'.

Collins was fond of old Mr Lucas, John the elder. Among the many occasions when he dined with him at Stouthall was a birthday party for Ann Powell on 27th November 1781; and on 28th May 1782 'Dined at Stouthall. Had 9 dozen and 11 bottles of port, part of a pipe of Mr Lucas's cask'. There were also parties given by the young Lucases at Fairyhill: '18 Feb 1785 went to Fairyhill. Dined and lay there. Lost at cards 1/-'. On 19th September 1787 Collins records the burial of 'my good old friend and neighbour Mr Lucas of Stouthall'. For a time the sociabilities with the young Lucases continued happily. On the 24th September 1789 there was the housewarming for the new parsonage at Oxwich: 'Mr and Mrs Lucas, Mr Jone etc. etc. dined on H of venison at Oxwich'. In 1793, on 12th May: 'Mr and Mrs Lucas drank tea. Mrs Lucas kindly offered to stand Godmother to my little boy'. During the next five months there were five occasions when Collins dined at Stouthall, including one when haunch of venison was on the menu. Once the gardener was sent over from Stouthall to Oxwich to advise Collins about his trees.

By 1794 there was a coolness between the families: '12th Sept Mrs Collins and self walked to Stouthall. Mr and Mrs Lucas not in the house or to be found. Saw the young gentlemen but could get no information. 4th Oct Received a note from Mr and Mrs Lucas with invitation to Dinner to-morrow. Not accepted'. On 15th June 1801 Collins complained that 'Mrs A. Collins received a note from Stouthall inviting her and daughter to dinner on Thursday, not a word to anyone else'. This does look rather an odd invitation — Collins himself had dined at Stouthall on June 2nd. There were further irritations, such as: '2nd Oct 1806 Went to view the road from Perryswood to Cold Comfort. Mr Lucas arranged to meet me, but did not. Came home wetted'. But there was friendship too: '1804 30th Jan Messrs Lucas, Cowell, Edwards and James dined and spent evening. Lost at cards 5/-. Very pleasant and merrie'.

In the summer of 1805 Collins brought trouble on himself. He proposed to his neighbours that they should in future call and see each other 'without ceremony or formal invitation' and proceeded to put his plan into effect, trying it out on Mr and Mrs Edwards: '29th August Mrs Collins, Fanny, Anstance and I dined at Brynfield uninvited. Great fuss'. Whether Edwards retaliated is not recorded, but soon afterwards the Collins family were rash enough to turn up at Stouthall uninvited, and spent the day there. The reaction was immediate, and the following week Collins wrote sadly: 'I find my plan not relished, and we received a severe reprimand from the Lucases by *Six of them coming on a Saturday at 2 o'clock to dinner* in return for our going at eleven o'clock one day to Stouthall and spending the day with them on a Monday. I intend in future to buy me some elegant paper or message cards and dispatch a messenger decently clad with formal invitations and Notices a day or two before we mean to make our approaches'.

The rebuff rankled and the following year Collins wrote to T. M. Talbot: 'Our visits to and from Stouthall are, as usual, rather formal than friendly which is always the case when etiquette is more regarded than social intercourse'. One suspects that John took rather a mischievous pleasure in taking a rise out of the Rector. It was in the same summer of 1805 that Joseph Green had written to Collins from London: 'Report here says that Mr Lucas has been so fortunate as to obtain £10 000 prize in the lottery. I hope you'll be able to confirm this news to me'. Collins called round at Stouthall, no doubt agog with interest, but came away disappointed. 'The report of Mr Lucas's fortune in the lottery has been whispered about in the neighbourhood', he wrote to Green, 'but not a hint from the family at Stouthall or any appearance of particular joy. Nay, I heard Mr Lucas complain much of the want of the yellow boys'. However local upsets were forgotten as news of the battle of Trafalgar began to trickle through: '8th Nov. News arrived of Lord Nelson's fleet raking and destroying 20 sail of the line combined fleet of Cadiz'. There was a victory celebration at Stouthall and the Collins were not left out: '26 Nov family and self went to Stouthall for dinner and ball. I came home with son John at three o'clock. 27 Nov family returned from Stouthall to a late dinner'. Sociability between the Lucas and Collins families continued until Collins's death in 1813, although with occasional tiffs, as in 1808 when Collins wrote testily of the Stouthall family that they were 'quite recluse'.

John Lucas the younger was a romantic, in the fashion of the time. He was also something of a dilettante with an interest in botany and natural history. It must have given him much satisfaction to be credited with the discovery of that charming little plant the yellow whitlow grass, *Draba aizoides*, whose shining yellow flowers peep cheerfully from crevices in the south Gower cliffs in the early Spring. Nowhere else in Britain does it grow wild. John found *Draba* growing 'near Worm's Head' in 1795 according to a footnote in Sowerby's *English Botany* of 1804. He also found it on the walls of Pennard Castle in 1805, so we are told by the Swansea botanist Lewis Weston Dillwyn. Ornithology was another of John's interests, and he helped to prepare the lists of birds recorded in the *Swansea Guide* of 1802.

John the younger's eldest son John Nicholas, known as the Colonel, was to inherit Stouthall, and to be the last male Lucas to live there. He was born in about 1784 and educated at Eton. In 1807 Mr Green the late tenant of Fairyhill was writing to Parson Collins: 'Is it true John Lucas junior is going to be married to a large fortune?' Collins replied: 'Reports are that the young squire is to be married to a Shropshire lady of Family and Fortune named Mackleton and the event was expected to have taken place ere this, but there has been some demur and delay; but it is generally supposed the event will take place — if Marriage Settlements etc can be properly adjusted'. But, alas, the fine adjustment of the finances seems to have come to grief and we hear no more of the young lady from Shropshire. Instead we find two Reynoldston girls claiming the young squire as father of their offspring; and his parents must have been relieved when a wife for him was eventually found, Mary Richards of Murton in Gower. There was no Marriage Settlement, and the absence of any Richards pedigree from the family archives suggests that Miss Richards did not possess what Collins meant by a Family. There is no evidence of Fortune either. The Colonel bought a property at Fairwood — he may have built it — called Killay Lodge, now Fairwood Lodge, but he was often away on military duty and his wife with him. It was at Aberdare in 1822 that his daughter Mary Catherine, known as Minnie, was born. Her mother died at her birth and in 1824 the Colonel remarried. His second wife was Letitia Tottenham the daughter of a former member of the Irish Parliament Nicholas Loftus Tottenham. The Colonel's second marriage was childless, and so it turned out that after three generations of 'heiress' marriages the owner of Stouthall was himself the father of an only child — or perhaps the only legitimate child — a daughter.

As a young man the Colonel helped to form an Association of Gower landowners known as The Gower United Association for the Prosecution of Felons, and his name heads the list of committee members elected at the inaugural meeting held in Llanrhidian in February 1810. The society aimed to combat the prevailing lawlessness of the times and to protect the property owner. A scale of rewards was offered for the arrest of malefactors; five guineas for footpads, burglars and arsonists; two guineas for cattle and poultry stealers and people found 'milking any cow or robbing a rabbit warren or any courtyard garden or orchard, plucking or stripping any sheep or lambs of their wool, dead or alive'. One guinea was to be paid for the arrest of dog stealers and destroyers of fences and hedges. Fifty-two Gower farmers and landowners were enrolled in the first year of the society. The first success came in 1812 when one D. Walters was prosecuted for stealing a pocket book from Mr Holland of Cwm Ivy. The legal process seems to have been pursued slowly but relentlessly, if one may assume that an entry in the accounts for 1814 'to recovery of Book from Bristol 0–1–8' relates to the same affair. The Committee met at the Inn of George Williams of Llanrhidian. There do not seem to have been a great many prosecutions but items such as 'to cash paid for Ale for the Committee 0–8–0' appear often in the accounts, and an Annual Dinner was started in 1823. The last reference to crime, a case of sheep stealing, comes in 1856 after which the activities of the society are confined to the Annual Dinner and payment of the Secretary's out-of-pocket expenses. These dinners were held at various public houses in Llanrhidian. In 1892 the members, now reduced to six, held their final celebration and the books were closed with a credit balance of twopence halfpenny.

Stouthall in 1840, the seat of Colonel Lucas

The Colonel did not long enjoy the status of Squire of Stouthall. He took possession on his father's death in 1831. Eleven years later his daughter Minnie married Edward Robert Wood who 'hung up his hat' at Stouthall, and the Colonel and his wife moved to Brynfield in Reynoldston where he died in 1863. We catch a last sight of him in a photograph taken in about 1860. He is seated in the family donkey car, well wrapped up against the cold. This donkey car was kept at Stouthall where it came in very useful for giving elderly relatives a breath of fresh air.

The Colonel's second wife Letitia had a sister Mary Tottenham who came to live with them at Stouthall. The story goes that this lady became passionately addicted to German bands and used to invite these itinerant musicians to come and play, and no doubt stay, at Stouthall. The Colonel could not stand them and on one occasion drove them from the house with the words 'Go and play on Cefn Bryn'; which they did, Miss Tottenham with them. I cannot vouch for this story, but it may well be that the Colonel did find his sister-in-law rather trying. It seems that he gave her his house Killay Lodge on the edge of Fairwood Common, presumably in the hope that she would go and live there. If she did so, it was not for long. By 1844 she had let Killay Lodge to a tenant and rejoined the Colonel and his wife at Brynfield.

It may be asked how the Colonel's daughter Minnie came to inherit Stouthall which was, as we know, entailed by her grandfather in 'tail male'. Under John the younger and Catherine's marriage settlement Stouthall would have passed, in the absence of male heirs for their eldest son the Colonel, to his younger brother Henry's surviving son the Rev. J. P. Lucas of Rhosili Rectory. Unfortunately for the latter, ingenious property lawyers had devised a method of avoiding the terms of a strict settlement of land. This involved a transfer of the property to a nominee, usually the family lawyer, followed by a fictitious law suit. Once the complicated formalities had been completed the land was freed from the entail and could be settled on fresh terms. It is hardly surprising that the Colonel with his father's agreement had set the legal wheels turning, and that as a result Minnie found herself as 'tenant for life' of the Stouthall estate which would afterwards go to her eldest child. My grandfather the Rev. J. P. Lucas was much upset by this breaking of the entail and as late as 1903 his widow and children went so far as to seek Counsel's opinion on the subject, cherishing a forlorn hope that part of the ancient patrimony might somehow, some day, come to them.

Going to market, Gower c.1840. From a Lucas family album.

4

1831–49
Henry Lucas the Racing Man
and his Children

In 1819 Colonel Lucas's younger brother, Henry IV, was married at Bath to Caroline one of the daughters of Ponsonby Tottenham a former member of the old Irish Parliament who had retired to live in Clifton. We have seen that a few years later the Colonel was to marry Caroline's cousin Letitia, daughter of another Tottenham, also an Irish MP. The Colonel's marriage to Letitia was childless but Henry and Caroline had seven children. Caroline Tottenham came from three influential families of the Anglo-Irish aristocracy, Loftus, Tottenham and Ponsonby. These three families were all of English origin, all Protestant, and all settled in Ireland by the middle of the 17th century. By the 18th century, the period of the Protestant Ascendancy in Ireland, they had amassed much wealth and were a powerful influence in Irish affairs. With their grand titles, their great estates in the Irish countryside, and their town houses in the elegant streets and squares of Georgian Dublin, they moved with ease and assurance in the highest ranks of society. Among them were distinguished soldiers, eminent politicians, Earls, Viscounts and Marquises.

It is not easy today to appreciate the importance attached by earlier generations to Rank and Family. This veneration for titled society shows particularly in the case of the Rev. J. P. Lucas for reasons which we shall discuss when we come to consider his character in a later chapter. Meanwhile we may safely assume that the Irish connection was a source of much quiet satisfaction at Stouthall.

Henry IV was a man of very different stamp from most of his forebears. The Gower Lucases had been mostly squires dedicated to their farms, conservative, parochial, perhaps rather puritanical in outlook. Henry by contrast was genial, debonair, sociable in taste and extravagant by nature, popular with his many friends but the despair of his family. His ruling passion was horse breeding and racing, whereby he dissipated a considerable fortune and left his children more or less penniless. One may wonder where the fortune came from. When Henry came of age in 1818 he would not have inherited much wealth from the Stouthall estate which was heavily in debt, and entailed on his elder brother. In fact Henry sold his reversionary interest to his sisters in 1828 for £430. His father was in no position to maintain him in any form of luxury. John the younger was himself in debt, like most of the gentry at that time, and in 1822 found himself in the embarrassing situation of being unable to pay his lawyer's bills which had by then accumulated to the formidable total of £1167. Henry's wife came of a wealthy family but she was one of ten sisters and not likely to have been endowed with much in the way of a fortune.

How then did Henry escape what was the usual fate of the younger sons of gentry families, the necessity of earning his living by going into the army or the Church or one of the professions? It is of course just possible that that fabled win of £10 000 in the National Lottery somehow found its way into Henry's pocket, but a more likely explanation is that his mother handed over to him her half share of the Powell Carmarthenshire property, which as we saw was separated from the rest of the estate by Act of Parliament. His father seems to have given him the Great House at Cheriton, and perhaps Fairyhill as well, but if his parents calculated that by financial generosity they would settle him down and give him an interest in estate management, they were disappointed. During the early years of their marriage Henry and Caroline lived at Dyffryn House beside the Llwchwr river at Ammanford in the Parish of Llandybie some ten miles south of Llandeilo. Here Henry would have been well placed to manage the Carmarthenshire properties. He may or may not have taken his duties seriously; all we know about this period of his life is that in 1820 he met with other like-minded gentlemen at Brecon to form an Association for the Protection of Game and Fish. His two eldest children were born at Dyffryn House, Henry Loftus Tottenham born in 1821 — known as Loftus but not to be confused with my father, another Loftus, born more than 40 years later — and Caroline Catherine born in 1822.

In 1823 Fairyhill fell empty on the death of the tenant, Lady Barham. This ardent supporter of the cause of Calvinistic

Caroline Lucas in 1830, aged 7   Henry Loftus Lucas in 1830, aged 8

Methodism, and mother of 22 children, had come to Gower in 1813 at the age of 50 and rented Fairyhill from the Stouthall estate. Estranged from her husband she devoted the rest of her life to the cause of Methodism in Gower. Within nine years she had built six churches, Bethesda at Burry Green, Bethel at Penclawdd, Trinity at Cheriton, Paraclete at Newton, Immanuel at Pilton Green and Mount Pisgah at Parkmill. She was an autocrat, and Ministers and Congregations were expected to toe the line. She herself worshipped at Bethesda, whither on Sundays she was borne by two flunkeys in a Sedan chair, across the fields from Fairyhill, to a room in the church known as Lady Barham's room, behind the pulpit. This room contained an elevated box pew entered by a flight of steps and belonged exclusively to the Fairyhill household. It also contained a fireplace, so that Her Ladyship was kept warm, though the rest of the congregation shivered. If Lady Barham tired of the sermon the door of the room was closed, and she went home. She died in April 1823, and an elaborate funeral procession wended its way right across the country to Kent where she was buried in the family vault at Barham near Canterbury. Henry and Caroline were quick to take possession of Fairyhill where on 30th October their third child John Ponsonby was born.

It seems that by now Henry had embarked on his hobby of training racehorses. Tradition says he had forty horses at Fairyhill. This may be exaggerated but no doubt the strings of horses exercising along the crest of Cefn Bryn must have become a familiar sight to the villagers at Reynoldston; but not for long. Henry soon tired of Fairyhill which was not very convenient for the Swansea race course on Crymlyn Burrows. Within a few years he had acquired, or perhaps built, a charming 'miniature mansion'

Henry Lucas, the racing man of the Uplands and Taliaris, by Dighton c.1830.

as a contemporary described it, at the Uplands, high on a hillside west of Swansea. Uplands Villa, as the house was called, was approached from what is now Cwmdonkin Drive. It stood four square on a narrow shelf of land projecting from the hillside, with lawns falling steeply from the south windows. The entrance with its classical portico faced east. On the west was a walled garden and pleasure grounds now called Cwmdonkin Park. Uplands was a gracious place with wide views over Swansea Bay and across the channel to the hills of Somerset. Here between 1825 and 1831 the next three children Maria, Louisa and Harriet were born.

Then Henry moved again, back to Carmarthenshire; not to Dyffryn House but to Taliaris that imposing and beautiful mansion in the hills north of Llandeilo where Richard Lucas from Fairyhill had lived as steward to the Gwynne estate in the early 18th century.

Taliaris was a place where Henry could hunt, shoot and farm to his heart's content while Caroline busied herself with domestic affairs and her growing family. What became of the race horses? One guesses that Henry kept them at Swansea, probably at stables convenient to the burrows east of the town. He retained Uplands Villa but showed little interest in his Gower property. The Great House at Cheriton was pulled down and a vague plan to rebuild it abandoned. Fairyhill had been put on the market. It was advertised in the *Cambrian* of 29th March 1828 as:

> A roomy family house about 12 miles from Swansea with good stables, coach house and a farm yard . . . a trout stream runs through the grounds. The remarkable fine sheep walk and extensive rights of common on the summit of which is a beautiful carriage road four miles in length, commanding the most romantic views, is near the premises . . . There is a sea port with excellent bathing about three miles off, where there is an oyster fishery, from whence they trade to Bristol, by which any commodities may be conveyed to the County.

The 'beautiful carriage road' is the track sometimes called Talbot's Road along the length of Cefn Bryn, traditionally constructed by Thomas Mansel Talbot of Penrice Castle, or possibly by his son who had inherited the Penrice Estate when he came of age in 1824. the 'sea port' must have been Porteynon.

It was at Taliaris that Henry and Caroline's youngest child Charlotte was born in 1833, only to die the following year. The two older children were by now at boarding school, Loftus at Llandeilo Academy and Caroline in Gower. Loftus had started school in Swansea when he was 9 years old. He achieved a prize before his tenth birthday, and this success drew a kindly letter of congratulation from his grandfather at Stouthall.

1st October 1830

My Dear Loftus,

Be assured it afforded me infinite pleasure to have the satisfaction of hearing of your obtaining a *prize* particularly so soon after your going to school; and I have no doubt of your proceeding in the same way, with diligent attention to your learning; for education and good principles make a *gentleman;* which I hope you will prove in every respect. I shall be very proud to be informed of your next success, and at all times of your progress in learning; and when you have a holiday I shall be very happy to see you here with your Papa.

With best love, my dear boy,

your ever affectionate grandpapa,

John Lucas.

Give my best love and many kisses to all your dear little sisters and to John, and tell him I hope he will follow your good example when he goes to school. My affectionate love to your Papa and Mamma, and a waistcoat is sent that was left here.

While Henry and Caroline were living at Taliaris, Loftus and his younger brother at Llandeilo Academy were close enough to receive fairly frequent visits from their parents. But an air of uncertainty seemed to hang over these visits — no doubt Henry was unpredictable. 'I suppose we shall go to see you' Loftus' mother would write, and again 'if it is fine I suppose we shall go. Let me know the hour.' Little Caroline in Gower was less fortunate. Her mother wrote to her from Taliaris on 1st April 1833, shortly before the child's eleventh birthday:

My dear little Caroline

I received yours of the 10th February after my patience was almost exhausted. I was very anxious to hear from you. Why do not you write to me much oftener? You must, Dear Child, let me hear every month or six weeks. I sent you half a quire of paper for writing home on, and a few sheets of letter paper on purpose for writing to Uncle Charles. You did not tell me what you said to him in answer for his kind presents to you. He likes proper

attention so I am very anxious you should write nice letters
to him. He is so very good to you that you must pay him
every mark of gratitude and regard you possibly can. Uncle
John and Aunt Letitia I was in hopes would long ago have
taken your things to you. Tell them with my love they have
so often disappointed us that we don't know how to depend
on them again, but that we hope when they do come that
they will make up for it by staying some time with us, not
as is their custom merely to say How d'ye Do and
Goodbye.

I think it best to keep your stuff frock till next winter,
Please God, as the summer may now be so soon expected,
and I suppose your coloured frocks are still good enough
for common. I send you two new white ones. I hope they
will fit you. I have had them made about two sizes larger
than an old one I had by me and a tuck for letting them
out to lengthen. Your new stays are sent belted in front
instead of the bone. I wish you had had them long ago as
your others I know were too tight. You must not wear the
others unless they can be let out sufficiently for you. Two
pockets are sent. You must change sides with them every
day for fear you should grow crooked. You must make
pocket holes in frocks and slips. I do not exactly remember
whether you wanted slips or no. I think you did. You will
let me know whatever you do want at any time and you
shall have them.

Your shoes are sent. I fear they are too small. If so do
not wear them but lay them by for little Maria against her
toots grow big enough and when you want shoes send me
the measure of your foot by just drawing a shape the length
of it in your letter. The width can be easily guessed by the
length. We have found out another shoemaker who makes
them better and cheaper than the Gower people so we
prefer him. I send a pair of stockings you left behind you,
and some belts etc also your bellows needle case stocked
with needles and pins and a new bodkin, some cotton and
some bobbins and a little Doll's portfolio with papers in it
for her to draw upon, and I hope you will prove a good
drawing mistress to her . . .

Even during the school holidays the parents were sometimes away,
and on one occasion her mother took Loftus with her; and
Caroline aged 12 or 13 was left in charge at Taliaris. Her mother
wrote:

Lion Inn, Builth
My dearest Caroline, Johnny, Maria, Louisa and Harriet
Here we are where we arrived last night very very tired.
As far as Llandovery I felt much refreshed, but the rest of

the journey, 23 miles more, fatigued me a good deal, and then the noise of the Inn and the heat of the room having been exposed to the evening sun kept me awake till near three o'clock in the morning. It was a most lovely day yesterday with a delightful breeze. I dont know what I should have done otherwise. But I hope by the time I get home again I shall be better altogether. We cannot be home tomorrow, I could not undertake the journey so soon again, but I hope either Friday or Saturday Please God! to embrace you all again.

The purport of this letter my dear Caroline is to tell you to mind in case there should be anything the matter with any of you that you dont know what to do, you will immediately send for Mr Prothero, writing him a nice note, well spelled and without blots or mistakes, saying what seems to be the matter, and to beg he will come if possible and to say I am at Builth. You will send first of all to Mrs Lewis's to ask if he is there or in the neighbourhood of Llandilo. If not send to his house. In my hurry I quite forgot to leave out some grains of his medicine for them, which I did intend to have done. Considering I had so little sleep last night I think myself tolerably well to-day. If Miss Ellen's boxes are not yet gone to Llandilo you should take off the hacking cloth, and tell Jane to put on in its stead the other half of the kitchen table cloth which she cut for Lewis the other evening. That hacking cloth *must not go at any rate*.

The post is going. I must say adieu. God bless you my dear Children. Kiss each other for me. Ever your most affectionate mother C. Lucas XX   Mind Caroline to tell Jane not to leave the children a moment. Loftus is quite in a rage because the people all seem to speak English. Mind Caroline you see every bit of butter weighed on Friday and write it all down. Loftus's love. He is in high spirits. I have just sent him to see Mrs Price. Did you ever see such paper with a gilt edge before.

Mrs Lucas's health, sadly, did not improve, and not long after this letter was written she died, on 1st September 1835, at the early age of 39 while on a visit to her sister in North Wales. She was buried 'in the Cathedral' at Bangor. Of her relations with Henry we know nothing, but from her letters it does seem that she tried to bring some order into his household. Her children loved her.

After his wife's death Henry gave up Taliaris and returned to Swansea. He had become friendly with a family called James, and it seems that Miss Caroline James was quick to take him on. In 1837 Loftus refers to her as 'Mamma'. Her step children did not like her and the family tradition is that she was foolish and vulgar. The re-marriage came at a particularly bad time for Caroline in her teens. By 1837 the boys had been moved from Llandeilo Academy to a new school, Mr Andrew's Academy at Ferryside. This village on the east bank of the Tywi estuary in Carmarthenshire with its wooded slopes and mild climate had become a fashionable seaside resort for the gentry. The boys were not happy there. They probably felt banished. In the autumn of 1837 Loftus was taken ill and had to be removed from school. At the same time his father suffered a bad accident, very likely a fall while hunting. Loftus was now 16. He wrote from his sick bed to Johnny who was two years younger:

40, Cambrian Place
Swansea

My dear Johney

I am happy to say that Papa is much better now than he has been, indeed he is now fast recovering. His head was so much brused by the fall that he could not speak for nine days. Dr Howel said that he thought he could never get well again and at last gave him over, but after he was cuped bled blistered and many other things he at last came to his senses, and is now getting better every day, but no one is allowed to see him but Mamma Uncle John and Uncle Bob. Dr Howel has been to see me every day since I have been here and I am geting better. I was put in a warm bath yesterday and am going in again to-morrow.

Please to send all my books clothes etc because next Wednesday I am going to England with Mr James to stay with him. How *delightful* . . . [paper torn] The name of the place is Marstoun about 30 miles beyond Bath. We are going next Wednesday in the packet. I do not want all my books only those I mention

My Latin English Dixionary	Classical Dixionary
English Latin do	Latin Grammar
Caesar	Readings in poetry
Eutropias	Arithmytic book
English Dixionary	Do coppy
Bible	Scripture history
Salust	Slate
History of England	Stuarts modern geography
History of Greece	Ancient Atlas
History of Rome	

and any other books I used to use that I may have forgotten to mention. The rest you may keep. Get all my cloths from Mrs Andrews my white troussers Shirts etc etc, pack them all in my long box and send them off immediately by the boat and then by mail. The direction you must put is Master Lucas 40 Cambrian Place Swansea. I suppose that you know that you are not to go back to Ferryside after this half of which I dare say . . . [paper torn] I must conclude as it is getting late. I hope you will not forget all my things and as soon as you get this letter if possible. If they do not come soon I shall be obliged to go without them, and that would be a bad job you know. I remain, my dear brother, yours affectionately, Loftus Lucas Aunts and Grandma send their love to you and I hope that you will make yourself comfortable till Christmas. PS if my cloths are dirty send them as they are . . [paper torn]

The letter is addressed to Master J. Lucas Ferryside nr Carmarthen. The Uncle John referred to is the Colonel. Uncle Bob is probably a James, perhaps the new Mrs Lucas's brother.

The sea voyage by packetboat from Swansea to Bristol was the quickest way of travelling between Swansea and southern England until the arrival of the railway at Swansea in 1850, although it was subject to delays caused by the weather. In 1837 there were three steam packetboats operating between Swansea and Bristol; the 'City of Bristol', the 'Pembroke' and the 'Palmerston'. They were paddle steamers, this being before the days of screw propulsion, and the owners described them, hopefully, as 'fast going'. In the summer months there were three sailings per week in each direction. The fare for passengers in the best cabin was 12 shillings, or six shillings and sixpence in the fore cabin, children half price. Steward service, with female stewards for the ladies, was one shilling extra. Livestock were carried as deck cargo. Sheep were one shilling and threepence, pigs one shilling and ninepence and dogs two shillings and sixpence each. Vehicles were taken at prices ranging from 16 shillings for a gig to 32 shillings and sixpence for a carriage and 17 shillings and sixpence for each horse. In 1840 the 'City of Bristol' was on a voyage from Waterford with 30–40 people on board including two women and a child, and a cargo of pigs, when she went aground on a stormy November night in Rhosili Bay. Next morning many of the pigs were found alive on Rhosili sands but apart from two men who managed to swim to safety every other soul on board was drowned. The remains of this ill fated ship are still to be seen at low tide between Diles Lake and Burry Holmes.

Loftus sounds a lively boy; one would like to know more of him.

But only a few months after writing the letter to his brother which I have quoted, he died at Uplands Villa, on the 12th March 1838, as a result of a hunting accident. One is left wondering whether he did manage to set off in the packetboat with Mr James, schoolbooks and all, on the visit he was so much looking forward to.

I now turn to Loftus's younger brother John Ponsonby, my grandfather, who was known in his youth as Johnny or Jacky. In 1838 he was taken away from Ferryside, as Loftus said would happen, and sent to a boarding school Bedminster House near Bristol. From here he wrote home at the age of 16 the following letter in an exemplary copper plate handwriting. The style is of such a chilling formality that I quote it as an example of how a schoolboy of the 1830s might be expected to write to his parents. I am glad to say that the epistolary style inculcated by Mr Goulstone had no effect whatever on my grandfather's adult mode of letter writing which was hasty, racy and vigorous.

Bedminster House
Dec 2nd 1839

My dear Parents,
    The happy time is arrived for me to address you on the subject of the Christmas vacation, which will commence on Thursday the 19th inst and terminate on Monday the 20th of January 1840. Since I have been at this Academy I have been daily endeavouring to improve myself in my studies which have been Latin, Greek, English Composition, Arithmetic and the Mathematics. I have read Horace Virgil and Livy alternately, and Herodotus in Greek, and I have nearly finished the first book of Euclid. I am happy to inform you that my Masters are perfectly satisfied with the progress I have made, and Mr Goulstone gives me permission to say my improvement has been general and conduct unexceptionable.
    I hope to have a letter from you soon, informing me when, and how, you wish me to return home.
    Mr and Mrs Goulstone desire me to present their respects to you. With best love to my dear sisters, and accept the same yourselves.
    I remain, dear Parents,
      Your dutiful son,
        J. P. Lucas.

With Loftus's death it was generally assumed, not least by my grandfather, that he would inherit his father's fortune and lead the life of a sporting country squire. His uncle Colonel Lucas encouraged him in this belief. 'I suppose,' he wrote to his nephew in 1839, 'you will hunt with the Swansea hounds when you come home. They have a large and good pack, and a great many gentlemen go out with them.' He also remarked to his nephew, in words which were never forgotten: 'It will all be yours one day, Jacky.' My grandfather took this to refer to Stouthall. Now all the grown-ups in the family knew perfectly well that the Stouthall estate had been re-settled on the Colonel's daughter Minnie. They had all joined in signing the legal documents; so what the Colonel meant is hard to say — perhaps he was talking about his brother's property. But Jacky saw himself as the future Squire of Stouthall. His father seems to have done nothing to encourage him to think differently, so when he left school he did not go to university or take any steps to fit himself for a career. Meanwhile Henry pursued the life of a well-to-do landowner. He farmed, he sat on the bench of Justices and with his brother took an active part in the suppression of the Rebecca disturbances in 1843. He was a Captain in the Swansea and Fairwood Cavalry. He hunted, and above all he raced his horses. In 1842 he was High Sheriff for the County of Glamorgan, a ruinously expensive honour as we have seen.

The inevitable financial crash came, it seems, in the late 1840s. All Henry's Gower properties, his farms in Carmarthenshire, Uplands Villa, even his first wife's jewellery were sold for his creditors. Henry left Swansea never to return and his children, now in their twenties, were, with the exception of Harriet who I believe stayed with her father, left to fend for themselves. I will say more about Caroline later. Maria married the warden of Llandovery School. Louisa married Pollet Cardew and emigrated to Australia where Harriet joined her and married William Cave. My grandfather, the hopeful young squire, did what was no doubt the most sensible thing in the circumstances; he returned to his studies, matriculated for Oxford University and in 1848 at the age of twenty-five went up to New Inn Hall, later part of Balliol College. He took his BA degree in 1851 and in the same year was ordained and found himself a penniless curate in the village of Tempsford by the banks of the River Ouse in Bedfordshire.

Henry had two children by his second marriage, a boy born in 1847 who died young and a girl Henrietta. Auntie Etta as she became known kept up with her half brothers and sisters. She lived in London. She was stoutish, down to earth, with a jolly laugh and just that hint of vulgarity which the Lucases, who so totally lacked it, found appealing. I have given the traditional view of Henry's character, and hope I have not done him an injustice. His happiest memories of Gower and Swansea must have been the horse races held annually on Crymlyn Burrows to the east of the town, where the Ford Motor Company's works now stand. W. H. Essery, in a manuscript in the Royal Institution of South Wales, remembers going to the races as a boy in about 1840:

> On a fine day it was really a gay and brilliant scene, many private four-in-hand drags being present, notably the magnificent turn-out of Mr Fredericks of Duffryn. Four of his grey pets, himself tooling them in a handsome carriage with a good swinging top-load of ladies and gentlemen, and a couple of well topped grooms in the rumble, were worth all the money.
>
> In those days many racing men from the English counties attended the Swansea meeting when on several occasions a goodly subscription provided valuable cups and stakes — Tom Parr amongst them — there were many local men too, such as Richard Douglas Gough, Henry Lucas, Charles Henry Smith, and sometimes the officers in charge of military. Mr Gough, like Mr Parr commonly rode his own horses, and well he did it, but his face and action in a close contest when nearing the post was a picture to behold. His eyes protruded as though they would outshoot the sockets, and his mouthing was fearful. It was all but momentary however for his features shortly resumed their usually placid form. A small black horse called Pilot ridden by himself won many races I remember.
>
> As a small boy, I have a vivid recollection of Mr Henry Lucas on one occasion winning a large and valuable cup, with a horse called Bay Hampton or Tottenham, I forget which. He had had ill luck and been constantly losing, and there was now great joy amongst his friends and the onlookers at his success, a joy not confined to them, but vastly appreciated by himself who, kind, amiable man as he was, came round to all the carriages with a servant carrying bottles of champagne, from which he from time to time filled his cup, with a request that each lady should drink his horse's health. One lady I know said 'I drink your health Mr Lucas,' when he at once checked her, saying 'No, my horse's health, if you please.'

5

The 1850s
Parson Lucas and the
Preacher's Daughter

Jacky, now the Reverend J. P. Lucas, was a Gower man at heart, and he can hardly have enjoyed his exile on the banks of the Ouse. It was by now obvious to him that he had no hopes of Stouthall where Colonel Wood had 'hung up his hat' or of any inheritance from his father whose wealth had vanished into the hands of his creditors. But it seems likely that during his short stay at Tempsford he met his future wife Rebecca Matthews who was then 16 years old and lived in Bedford with her brothers and sister, and widowed mother. Rebecca was the daughter of the Reverend Timothy Richard Matthews of Bedford. The Matthews family originated from Norwich where they were prominent in local affairs during the latter part of the 17th and the 18th centuries. Timothy Richard was born in 1795, the eldest of 14 children of whom all but four died in infancy. His father was Rector of the fenland village of Tydd St Giles, a rich living said to be worth £1500 a year. Young Timothy Richard received a good education and early in life developed a flair for speaking in public. At the age of 14, while at Grammar School in Norwich, he recited Gray's *Elegy Written in a Country Churchyard* before the assembled school, with great effect.

In 1815 Timothy Richard entered Sidney Sussex College, Cambridge. At this period of his life he enjoyed fishing, shooting, skating and music. It was during his undergraduate days at Cambridge that Matthews came under the influence of a famous evangelical preacher, the Rev Charles Simeon, fellow of King's College and perpetual curate of Holy Trinity Church in Market Street. This Church already had a tradition of eminent 18th century Divines who sought to illuminate the Christian way of life by the two lights which God had given, the light of Reason and the light of

Scripture. On Friday evenings Matthews and other like-minded undergraduates, sometimes 40 or more of them, would repair to Simeon's rooms over the archway in the Fellows Building at King's. Here in his drawing room overlooking the great west lawn and the banks of the Cam, Simeon would sit on an unbacked chair by the fireplace propounding and discussing difficult texts of Scripture with the rows of students seated on forms in front of him. These 'Friday men' as they were called would attend Holy Trinity Church for the Sunday services. Matthews would sit enthralled among the packed congregation as Simeon in the pulpit declaimed the vision of the prophet Isaiah with the utmost passion and fervour. Despite his strange gestures — he would stand in the pulpit with outstretched arm, flicking the top of his thumb with his forefinger as if, it was said, he was trying to catch a fly — Simeon's influence on the more serious-minded undergraduates was profound.

Matthews graduated in 1818, was ordained priest, and appointed to the curacies of Colmworth and Bolnhurst, two country villages a few miles north of Bedford on the Kimbolton road, at a stipend of £100 per annum with use of the Rectory. Here he was greatly influenced by a woman of strong character and religious faith, Mrs Rachel Fielding, the wife of a local farmer and Methodist preacher. The Fieldings had two daughters, noted for their beauty, and it was not long before Matthews had fallen in love with Ann Fielding the elder of the two. They were married in 1821, despite the opposition of Matthews's father, who viewed his son's evangelical and Methodist leanings with alarm. Not long after the marriage Matthews's parents died; and Matthews was offered the living of Tydd St Giles. To exchange a curacy of £100 per annum for a Rectory worth £1500 per annum must indeed have been a sore temptation for a newly married curate, and he was much urged by his friends to make the change. But he refused saying merely that if he was blessed with children, God would provide for them.

Yet Matthews was at this time troubled by doubt and uncertainty about his religious calling. He had begun his ministry by reading his father's sermons from the pulpit. But how dull he found them, how unevangelical; so unlike the sermons of Mr Simeon! And his congregations remained small and apathetic.

One day when he was praying alone in Colmworth Church 'there fell as it were scales of darkness from his eyes, and bright heavenly light burst upon him. He saw that his sins were forgiven, freely blotted out in the atoning blood of Christ; he saw himself reconciled to God'. He hurried home and exclaimed to his wife: 'I have found that which I was so long seeking; now I know what it is to be a child of God'. Matthews resolved that he must not only minister to his own people, but also to 'sinners perishing in the neglected parishes around him'. This he would do by open-air preaching. He threw away his father's sermons and began writing his own. There was no lack of 'neglected sinners' for in those days the fox-hunting parson was the rule rather than the exception. Matthews soon gave up Colmworth and Bolnhurst and became Chaplain at the Bedford workhouse, or House of Industry as it was called. He and Ann made their home at the old Grey Friars Priory in Bedford. He eked out his slender salary by coaching private pupils in the classics.

During the 1830s Matthews was preaching to ever-increasing congregations at the chapel of the House of Industry, in the streets and squares of Bedford, and in the surrounding towns and villages. People flocked to him. In his preaching he exercised a strange magnetic power over his hearers. He would arrive, wearing his black gown and bands, in the street or marketplace, stand on a chair or stool — he was a man of tall and commanding appearance — and gather people to him by blowing his trumpet. He had a silver trumpet and horn and also a bugle, which are still preserved. It was said that in church or chapel on the rare occasions when he observed any member of the congregation dozing off, a stentorian blast on the bugle would arouse the startled sleeper in the conviction that the last trump was indeed sounding.

Matthews's fervour and his unconventional preaching aroused fierce opposition and hostility from the 'establishment'. He could expect neither sympathy nor understanding from men like the Reverend Gustavus Burnaby, the jovial Rector of St Peter's, Bedford who, it was said, allowed his wife to write his sermons, kept dustpans and brushes under the communion table, hats in the font, and washing drying in the churchyard. There was a campaign of ridicule and vilification against Matthews. His children were sneered at and had to find their way to school by back streets. The press reported such items as: 'Matthews . . . has during the last few days been blowing his tin horn at Riseley with three or four women at his heels, and announcing that he was blowing the last trump, and that our Saviour would shortly descend on a stack of barley which was standing near.' Influential people in Bedford managed to close the chapel at the House of Industry thinking that they would thereby deprive Matthews of a base. But within 19 weeks his

congregation had built for him a large church in the Bromham
Road, with living quarters for his family. The building was known as
Christchurch and in later years called the Bromham Road Chapel.
Here the preacher's popularity increased still more. The Bishop
refused to license the Church, so Matthews continued regardless,
calling his ministry the Primitive Episcopal Church or the Reformed
Church of England, and maintaining his own register of Baptisms
and Burials. He set great store by Baptism by Total Immersion,
often in the River Ouse. On Easter Sunday 1842 he held an early

Reverend T. R. Matthews, c.1840.

morning service by the river at which 150 people were present. 'A little while before I baptised', he wrote, 'the sun had risen with peculiar splendour; his bright rays threw a lustre over the solemn scene, and met the faces of our baptised brethren and sisters as they came out of the water, making their faces sparkle again, as the dew-drops in the morning sun. It was a glorious time — the sun shining, the children of God rising out of the water, the animated voices of friends by the riverside, singing "Glory Honour Praise and Power" made the whole scene truly solemn.'

By the early 1840s Matthews had extended his preaching and pastoral work far afield, to Manchester, Liverpool, Birmingham, Leicester, London and Brighton. In all these places he was welcomed by large congregations. It was estimated that on one occasion at Leicester 5000 people assembled to hear him preach in the open air. At Bedford his enemies faded away and he became very popular with the townspeople. An occasional attender at Matthews's services at Christchurch was the poet Edward Fitzgerald, whose brother John was one of Matthews's most staunch supporters. Edward himself, although not a believer, found Matthews fascinating. 'My noble preacher' he called him. The poet describes the scene in the Bromham Road on Good Friday 1844 when the crowds waiting outside the chapel to hear Matthews preach filled the road and stopped the traffic. His sermon was on the crucifixion, the church was packed and many were turned away. Fitzgerald wrote:

> . . . at the end of his grand sermon Matthews called on some of the people to say merely this, that they believed Christ had redeemed them; and first one got up and, in sobs, declared she believed it, and then another — I was quite overset — all poor people. How much richer than all who fill the London Churches! Theirs is the Kingdom of Heaven . . . Oh this wonderful world! And we who stand in the middle of it are all in a maze, except poor Matthews of Bedford, who fixes his eyes upon a wooden cross, and has no misgivings whatsoever.

Mr and Mrs Matthews had five children, Benjamin, Joseph, Timothy (often known as Richard), Ann and Rebecca. Mrs Matthews shared her husband's life completely. He wrote to her after they had been married for ten years: 'The gold of Peru is nothing compared to what I possess in you . . . dearest kindest and best of wives, I pray and bless the Lord for you every day.' Mrs

Matthews sometimes accompanied her husband on his pastoral journeys, and on these occasions the two youngest children Ann and Rebecca were left in the care of a member of their church, Miss Timaeus, who kept a children's boarding school. The far-off world of Miss Timaeus and the boarders comes across to us touchingly in Rebecca's Prayer. It is dated December 18th 1840, when she was 5 years old:

> O God bless me and my sister and make us both good girls, and God bless my dear brothers. Let them love each other and not disagree but let Joseph love Timothy and let Timothy love Joseph and let them be good and happy and let them come to you when they die. Bless Papa and Mamma and let them go to Heaven when they die and let us be good children and do as we are bid and not stay but go directly. Let us play but not on Sunday, but mind what Papa and Mamma say to us. God keep Miss Timaeus and all the Boarders and bring us all together again and let them all live and be good and happy and let them come to you O God when they die, and let me be a good girl and say my piece very nicely and not cry and then sit down as I did this breaking up, and bless Miss Vines and Miss Timaeus and all the Boarders.

Matthews's sermons and pastoral letters and many of his letters to his children have been carefully preserved. They show him as being totally obsessed with the spiritual welfare of his correspondents. Almost every sentence is an exhortation against sin; to follow the path of righteousness; and to prepare for the second coming of Christ on earth. Even his natural concern for the health and welfare of his children — Matthews was a devoted father — is expressed in spiritual terms. 'Sometimes Satan harasses me very much about you . . . I am afraid he should lead my dear Boy into some temptation . . . I sometimes fancy that you might be tempted in fishing to go too near the edge of the sluices and fall in, or to venture on the sand and get swallowed up in a sand-pit.' But Matthews was in no way exclusive or bigoted. He never tried to frighten people to mend their ways out of fear of hell fire or damnation. His message was always of the love and joy to be found in the Christian way of life. He was entirely without hatred or guile; he worked for reconciliation between the Church of England and Methodism and he was on close and friendly terms with the Jewish communities in Bedford and London; he was careful to speak to his hearers in simple language and in terms

which would be easily understood by the poor and ill-educated.
Children were greatly attracted to him. To hear him speak was an
emotional experience. He once described the scene at the
conclusion of one of his open-air Sunday evening sermons:

> Hundreds flocked round me, four or five shaking me by the
> hand at once. Men women and children — some with tears
> in their eyes — some saying 'You must not go yet; you
> should stop: where do you live? The Lord bless you'. All
> the way up the street they followed me, shaking hands with
> me and blessing me, till I was glad to take shelter in a
> friend's house.

Matthews had a pony and gig which he used for many of his
journeys. One of the very few mundane affairs to receive a
mention in his letters was his care and concern for the pony. 'The
pony performed her journey with ease, and appeared but little
tired; I have just been to see her and she is eating away. Mr Waters
said to the servant "Let her have what corn and hay she likes".' In
1845 he writes to his sons Joseph and Timothy with directions for a
journey from Bedford to Burnham. After exhortation to prayer
and scripture reading he concludes with some practical advice:

> Hold a tight rein. Go gently down hill. Walk up steep hills.
> Use the whip but little. In meeting carts etc be sure to turn
> out in time, and keep the pony out, as she is apt to turn
> towards the cart too soon. Now and then see whether her
> shoes are all on. At March put up at the White Hart Inn,
> near to Aunt's house. See the pony at eight o'clock. Her
> feed, corn and beans. Hay at night. See her fed on Sunday
> morning with the same feed . . . Feed on Monday morning
> the same, but be sure to see her fed, and let her have at
> least half an hour to eat it in.

By the early 1840s Matthews was wearing himself out with
continual travelling and preaching up and down the country. In
three years (1841–43) he preached no fewer than 1008 sermons,
almost one a day. During this time the only relaxation he allowed
himself was music. His instrument was the violin; and sometimes
his tame canary would sit perched on the bow while he played. In
August 1845 he undertook an exhausting tour in and around
London, although he was far from well. On 23rd August he
travelled back to Bedford on the outside of *The Times* coach. He
appeared so ill that the other travellers became alarmed for his
safety. On reaching home he at first refused to see a Doctor; and
he managed to fulfill one final engagement, a burial service on

August 25th. But it became plain to his family and to the Doctor who was eventually summoned that Matthews was dying, and the end came on 4th September. As John Wesley would have said he 'died well', surrounded by his wife and children. He was aged 50. His widow later recorded an affecting account of his last hours.

Reverend J. P. Lucas, Rector of Rhosili. Copied from an Ambrotype, a positive on glass backed by varnish, popular in the 1850s and early 1860s.

I now return to my grandfather the Reverend J. P. Lucas, whom we left as a newly ordained curate at Tempsford in 1851. He did not remain long in Bedfordshire, and held two more curacies, at Whitworth in Shropshire in 1853 and Fladbury near Evesham in Worcestershire in 1854. Meanwhile some changes were taking place among the Gower clergy, and we may be sure that my grandfather kept abreast of what was happening. The Reverend John Lloyd had been Rector of Rhosili since 1838. The parsonage house was in a dilapidated state and Mr Lloyd at first found it more convenient to lodge in Rhosili village and let the parsonage to a farmer, Mr Lewis, who patched it up and lived there with his family. At this time the living of Llangennith was held by the Reverend Samuel Phillips whose home was at Fairyhill, he having married Julia, one of Lady Barham's numerous offspring. Phillips resigned Llangennith in 1852 and Lloyd took it on in addition to Rhosili. For the next two years Lloyd held both parishes, and it seems likely that this is when the parsonage, at the foot of Rhosili Down, was rebuilt; for Lloyd's convenience, it being at least part of the way to Llangennith. But in 1854 Lloyd moved to the vacant living of Oxwich. His eyesight was failing and no doubt Oxwich was altogether more manageable for him than Rhosili and Llangennith. The result was a vacancy in the two westernmost parishes of Gower, with a modern Rectory ready for occupation. The snags, from the point of view of many young parsons and still more parsons' wives, would have been the remote situation of the villages, the isolation of the parsonage house, almost inaccessible except on foot or on horseback, and the gross annual income of no more than £174. But for my grandfather it was a wonderful opportunity to return to his homeland. He applied; was accepted, perhaps with a little luck and family influence with the Bishop of St David's; and in February 1855 he was formally instituted as Rector of Rhosili and Vicar of Llangennith. He moved in to the parsonage house with his Aunt Harriet Lucas to keep house for him.

What were the Rector's thoughts on that winter's day in 1855 as he journeyed out from Swansea, 18 long miles of muddy Gower roads to Rhosili, passing the lanes and crosses leading to so many old Lucas family houses — Uplands Villa, Fairwood Lodge, Stouthall, Fairyhill, Brynfield, the ruins of the Great House at Cheriton — all lost to him through the accident of birth or his father's extravagance? I am sure he felt that fate had been unkind. Yet his journey's end was to be a place of such rare quality, a land and seascape so compellingly beautiful that few can first come upon it without a lift of the heart, a catch of the breath.

I so well remember my own first sight of Rhosili, on a summer evening in 1926 when I was 10 years old. We had come for the holidays and after the train journey from Paddington to Swansea came the long slow grinding drive through Gower in the Vanguard motor bus. Then quite suddenly the western sky was glowing with light and we had arrived, in a moment of astonishing climax, at the world's end. There was a huddle of cottages perched on top of a cliff, on the edge of an empty expanse of sea and sky, shining in the evening light. To the left were steep cliffs, and beyond them, reaching far out into the sea, was the strange black outline of the Worm's Head. To the right Rhosili Down loomed above the village, and slopes of tangled gorse and bracken plunged dramatically down towards the sea. Far below, and infinitely remote, the wide empty sands of Rhosili Bay stretched northwards into the distance. There was no wind. On the sea a slow ocean swell came crawling out of the sunset, and broke into broad white bands along the rim of the bay. The air was filled with an undercurrent of sound, the steady roar of the surf. As the years passed, and holidays came and went, Rhosili revealed new beauties; the grey bleached limestone cliffs; the perfection of sand and rock in Mewslade and Fall; the fierce excitement of winter gales with the

The old Rectory at Rhosili, photographed by Harold Grenfell.

crash of Atlantic rollers sending vast sheets of spray up and over the cliffs at Thurba, stinging across the rocks at Tears Point, quivering into the eye of the wind at the far end of the Outer Head. Then there were the flowers; spring primroses and cowslips growing along the lanes and under the hedgebanks; foxgloves in June; the cliffs speckled with rockroses, and the misty drifts of pale blue scillas in May; and always the warm sweet scent of the gorse and the tang of the sea on soft blue days after rain.

When my grandfather came to Rhosili in the middle of the 19th century the road from Swansea as far as Pitton Cross was for the most part a wide indeterminate strip of land between fields and across commons, along which the carts and waggons would pick their way, raising clouds of dust in summer and in the winter skirting round the deep ruts and pools. After Pitton Cross the road contracted into a narrow lane between hedgebanks and stone walls just wide enough to take a horse and cart. Through Middleton the lane took on the appearance of a farmyard. Here was a hamlet of some ten or a dozen cottages, whitewashed, two-storey, with tiny square upper windows and roofs of slate or thatch. There were stone porches to the front doors and sometimes a tiny front garden enclosed by a wall which was limewashed white, like the houses. Chickens and geese pecked in the gutter; there were farm carts creaking and the jingle of harness. A few gnarled elms gave welcome shade in the summer, and moaned in the winter gales.

The houses ended at the Ship Inn and the narrow lane continued between high hedge banks for half a mile to Rhosili. Here, scattered on either side of the church, was another group of some eight or nine cottages. One single tree grew in the village, an ash tree in a farmyard by the church. Inhibited by the salt-laden wind from the sea the tree grew horizontally across the farmyard, no higher than the top of the wall between the farmyard and the road. In the springtime primroses flowered in the hedgebanks and pennywort grew in the crannies of the walls — the children called it Catty-sit-upon-the-wall and rubbed the juice into their boots to make them squeak when they walked up the aisle in church on Sunday; like new boots. At the western end of the village a track led out on to the cliff and the last cottage, Harepits, was almost on the cliff edge. To the north of the village a lane led from the green to the south side of Rhosili Down where there were some wells and stone troughs. From this point a rough footpath continued round a bluff and across the steep seaward face of Rhosili Down. The path was rocky and uneven, and crossed by small streams trickling down the hillside. After a gradual descent of about half a mile the path arrived at Rhosili Rectory, the only building in the huge expanse of Rhosili Bay. Immediately behind the Rectory the hillside rose steeply, almost precipitously, some 450 feet to the top of the Down, while in front a gently sloping meadow led down to the edge of a low cliff and the empty expanse of sand and sea. Beyond the Rectory to the north the path ran level and after about a mile reached another lonely house, Hillend, set back a little from the sea, round the northern end of the Down. From Hillend lanes led for half a mile into Llangennith village.

How did the Rectory come to be built in this romantic situation? It was not, as is sometimes supposed, originally intended to serve both parishes. Llangennith at one time had a parsonage of its own. The reason why the Rectory and the church glebe land lay at the foot of the Down, between the hillside and the sea, was that this was the site of the early medieval village. The remains of the little 12th century church may still be seen among the sandhills below the modern village, and the foundations of a contemporary house have recently been excavated beside this old church; also what was once the wall of the churchyard. It seems likely that this early settlement was besanded during the 13th century, causing the villagers to move up to the present village site on top of the cliff, taking with them, according to tradition, the fine old church doorway which they built into their new church on the cliff.

The builders of the 19th century Rectory chose the site of a much earlier building part of which was left more or less intact at the back of the new house. The new Rectory was well and solidly built. The materials must have been brought by horse and cart along the rough track from the village. This old cart track ran in the shelter of a high stone wall built along the top of the glebe fields. It was impassable on foot and for much of its length it formed the bed of a stream. It was scarcely usable in my grandfather's time and visitors to the Rectory had perforce to go on foot along the path already described, which ran a little higher up the hillside. There was then no road from Rhosili village down to the burrows.

The architect who designed the 19th century Rectory seems to have paid little regard to convenience in such an exposed situation. The front door faces due west out to sea, and the back door due south out of the kitchen. In neither case is there any porch to mitigate the tearing wind and driving rain. The Rectory was thus briefly described by the diocesan surveyor in 1898:

> The buildings consist of a Vicarage House and offices,
> another detached block of old buildings consisting of a back
> kitchen with floor above. There are also outbuildings
> detached, consisting of a beast house, coal house, stable,
> chaff room, pigscot and yard, forming one block of
> building. The walls of all buildings are built of stone. The
> roofs of the Vicarage house and offices, stable, chaff room
> and pigscot are covered with slate. The roofs of the back
> kitchen, beast house and coal house are covered with straw
> thatch. There are two plots of garden ground having a
> stone wall around each.

The front door of the house led into a central hall or passage with doors leading off into the two front rooms, dining room on the right and drawing room on the left. Behind the dining room on the south side of the house was the kitchen, the largest room in the house, and at the back was a long narrow and dark dairy. To reach the first floor you could either use the front stairs just inside the front door, or the back stairs which consisted of a spiral iron staircase rising out of a little cupboard room behind the drawing room. Upstairs were two front bedrooms, a nursery over the kitchen, a store room over the hall and a very small spare room. The old detached building at the back contained a fireplace and a copper for doing the family wash. There was no bathroom but china washbasins in the bedrooms and a metal bathtub which could be brought out and used in front of the kitchen fire. The toilet or privy was a small stone building in the yard with a wooden seat and bucket. Water came from a spring on the hillside. The Rector fitted up a pipe which led from the spring to a storage tank at the back of the house.

Rhosili Rectory was to be the home of the Rev J. P. Lucas and his wife and family for over 40 years. When he first moved in as a bachelor with his Aunt Harriet the Rectory was commodious for the two of them and a servant maid. They brought with them various bits and pieces of furniture from Stouthall and Uplands Villa. Aunt Harriet was a keen gardener and set about making formal flower beds in front of the house. Here was a brave show of crocuses in the spring, and in the summer nasturtiums battled against the endless salt winds. Pots of cyclamen and geraniums grown from seed appeared in the front windows. Indoors the family ancestors were assembled in their gilded oval frames on the walls of the dining and drawing rooms. Here was John the younger, an elegant young man, slight of build, with fine features, grey eyes, and the corners of his mouth pursed with a touch of obstinacy; his wife Catherine and sister-in-law Anne, two frail young ladies, wistful and delicate in the high fashion of late 18th century Bath; and John's mother-in-law Catherine Powell, pretty and sparkling, a little brassy perhaps — so flatteringly captured, it is said, by the young Thomas Lawrence who while still in his teens was living in Bath and 'fully employed in taking crayon likenesses of the fashionables of the place at a guinea or a guinea and a half a head'. Here too was the handsome girl with the brown eyes and flicker of a smile, reputed to be John's mother Hannah the heiress of the Nicholas family fortune. These ancestors were joined by the Rector's father Henry IV, in a bird's eye maple frame, sketched in profile by Dighton probably around 1830. We see him smart and debonair, with a twinkle in his eye and his arms clutched to his chest in enjoyment of a joke.

One may be sure that the Rector relished the opportunity to farm part of the glebe land. Most of it was let, but he kept several fields for his own use. He acquired a cow, a few pigs, and a flock of sheep, and, in later life, a horse. Farming as we have seen was in his blood. An old Gower farmer once told me: 'I remember my mother showing Parson Lucas her sewing machine, the first ever in Gower. "Very clever," he said after examining it closely, "but I'd rather have a chaff cutter."' Rhosili was a parish of farmers and smallholders. In the 1870s, when the population was no more than 270 there were some 27 families with farms of five acres or more. The largest farm was Great Pitton with 250 acres and there were a further eight farms of around 50 acres. Almost everyone was a tenant of the Penrice estate.

In the 1850s the parish had a slowly declining population. There were the reasons common to most country districts, agricultural depression, the coming of the railways and the attraction of industry, and emigration to the colonies and the New World. A particular cause of decline in Rhosili was the ending of the limestone trade; for many years the cliffs in Rhosili and elsewhere in Gower had been quarried. At Rhosili the limestone was loaded into boats at the foot of the cliffs between the village and the Point, and exported to ports along the south coast of the Bristol Channel. By the 1850s this coastal trade had been killed by the railways. The quarries in the cliffs fell silent and the herring gulls and ravens returned to their traditional nesting places.

For the new Rector the Parish posed two major problems. One was the fabric of the church itself, which had fallen into a sorry state. A drawing done in September 1855 by the Rector's sister Cathy shows the roof ridges sunk below the gable ends — possibly the roof had been thatched — the crude window openings in the nave, and the soil from the churchyard piled against the walls, making the interior intolerably damp. The nave floor was bare clay and the chancel floor was pebbled. Rain dripped through the roof and ran down the walls. Once a year at Easter it was the custom to give the church a vigorous coat of whitewash, inside and out. This may have masked for a time the worst symptoms of decay, but it led Dr Freeman, a well-known authority on church buildings, to observe in 1850 that the Norman doorway was 'so grievously defaced with whitewash that the design of its capitals cannot be ascertained'. There was little money to be had but the Rector lost no time in doing urgent repairs to the roof and fabric. The work was started in September 1855.

The second problem was more intractable and one which my grandfather was by temperament ill-fitted to deal with. It was what one might describe as the spiritual division of the village into two opposing camps, Church and Chapel. Dissent from the established Church had been strong in Gower since the 17th century. In Rhosili it may be traced to 1650 when the Rector Edward Gamage was removed by Parliament from the living and replaced by a Cromwellian minister Daniel Higgs. This man Higgs became very unpopular with some local people, and after the restoration of King Charles II in 1661 Higgs was expelled from Rhosili, being 'forced to leave his wife and seven children to avoid the fury of the mobb'. Eventually 'when the storm was blown over' Higgs became pastor to a dissenting congregation in Swansea. Gamage was reinstated, but the storm over Higgs rumbled on and there was continuing trouble in the village between Church people and nonconformists. In the 1660s legal proceedings were brought by the Church authorities against some Rhosili people for failing to attend church and refusing to pay the church dues. In 1668 and 1669 the Rector declined to write up the church registers because the fee of three shillings and eightpence was unpaid.

By an Act of 1689 the penalty for non-attendance at church was abolished. Thereafter nonconformists were free to attend their own place of worship, but with the sanction removed the church people too were inclined to stay away, and congregations declined. Furthermore the nonconformist farmers still had to pay their tithes to the Rector and this was a continual source of friction. Throughout the 18th century dissent took deeper root in the village and Methodism flourished, although the clergy in their reports tended to play down this challenge to the authority of the established Church. In 1831 or thereabouts the Beynon family at Great Pitton farm, where 'Wesley's Chair' is still preserved, allowed a Wesleyan Methodist chapel to be built on their land in the lane leading to the farmhouse. When my grandfather became Rector of Rhosili this chapel was crowded with worshippers on Sundays, and the lower Pitton valley was filled with the strains of vigorous hymn singing. At Rhosili church by contrast the congregation was small and their devotions appeared apathetic.

Despite the deep-rooted causes of sectarian intolerance the problem in Gower villages was not insoluble. At Llanmadoc and Cheriton the Reverend J. D. Davies, a High Church Ritualist, succeeded in filling his churches and at the same time retaining the respect and affection of the chapel. At Rhosili my grandfather was less successful. Inclined by temperament to retreat into his shell when opposed, he resolved to meet what he saw as a challenge to the authority of the established church by ignoring it. He would not or could not bring himself to have an easy relationship with those whom he regarded as opponents. Hence his reputation among Gower people who did not know him well as a proud remote sort of man; while in his own small circle he was loved and respected. But it was indeed a fortunate day both for my grandfather and for the people of Rhosili when, on the 10th November 1857, he married Rebecca Matthews the younger daughter of the preacher. The wedding was in Reynoldston church where the bride's brother the Reverend Richard Matthews conducted the ceremony, and another brother Dr Benjamin Matthews gave his sister away. This Dr Matthews after some years as medical officer at Bedford asylum and later as a ship's surgeon, was now in practice at Reynoldston where his wife had given birth to a baby daughter, and Rebecca had come to help manage the house.

This union of Lucas and Matthews brought together at Rhosili Rectory two families of vastly different backgrounds; the Rector and his aunt (who stayed on at the Rectory until her death in 1867) imbued with the ancient traditions of the Gower Squires; and the Rector's young wife, pious, practical and competent, a woman of the people whose East Anglian evangelism struck a responsive chord in the hearts of the villagers of west Gower — although she was the only person living in Rhosili parish whose place of birth was further afield than Swansea. But before we go on to look at life at Rhosili Rectory, we must return to the Rector's sister Cathy.

6

1850–80
The Wilkinsons and Lady Llanover

The Rector and his wife, in their secluded parsonage by the edge of the sea, were isolated by Rhosili Down and 18 miles of Gower fields and commons from the very different world which began at Swansea. South Wales in the 1850s was still in the throes of industrial development. Along the heads of the south Wales valleys, from Hirwaun to Blaenavon, stretched a chain of ironworks. Those at Dowlais and Cyfarthfa with their complex of coal mines, factories and furnaces were the largest producers of iron in the world. Along the steep-sided valleys of the Taff and Cynon rivers, and from the mountain sheep walks of the Rhondda, the train loads of steam coal rumbled down to the docks at Cardiff. On the 18th June 1850 the first railway train from Cardiff puffed and clanked into Swansea station. By the mid 1850s, in a few square miles of the lower Swansea valley, there were two ironworks, two tin-plate factories, seven coal mines, and ten copper-smelting works producing over half of the world's supply of copper; and a number of minor works and factories. Here the black and yellow smoke belching from a hundred chimneys hung in a pall which blotted out the sunshine and by night reflected the flickering green flames of the copper furnaces. The pollution was such, so it was said, that not a plant, not a blade of grass would grow on the side of Cilfai hill.

Swansea itself was a town of contrasts. Down by the seashore the town still had some pretensions to be a holiday and health resort, although the delights of a broad sandy beach 'admirably adapted for sea bathing' were considerably modified by the 'smoke and noxious effluvia' which so often drifted across it. In the Burrows were the Assembly Rooms, the Royal Institution of South Wales, and the faded Regency houses where, in their palmier days, Catherine

Lucas, widow of John the younger, had passed her declining years. Now rows of lodging and apartment houses sought the trade of the summer visitors. But inland, not more than a short walk from the beach, were scenes of appalling squalor. In large areas of the town there was no piped water and no sewers. Groups of houses shared a communal privy which was often little better than a hole in the ground, and obtained their drinking water from shallow and polluted wells. In the Greenhill part of the town near the High Street Station sewage and filth lay piled in the narrow alleys. Two-roomed houses, lacking in any sort of amenity, were still being built in the 1850s. In each such house, clustered round tiny courts, lived families of six or eight people. Epidemic diseases were rife and caused one third of all deaths among the working class population. From time to time cholera ravaged the poorer quarters.

But to the west of Swansea, if you walked only a mile or two out of town, the contrast was startling; the air was pure and sweet, the countryside green and unspoiled, the sea views enchanting. Here lived the wealthy families, the big industrialists and landowners. Singleton Abbey, an elaborate house built in 1823 in Singleton Park, was the home of John Henry Vivian the Cornishman who made his fortune in the copper industry. At Sketty Hall lived Lewis Weston Dillwyn, a man of learning and culture, an eminent botanist, who once owned the Cambrian potteries in Swansea. His son John Dillwyn Llewellyn lived at Penllergaer. He too was a botanist and, with his famous cousin Fox Talbot, a pioneer of the early photographic processes. In the Clyne valley George Warde, soldier and coal owner, had built his Gothic mansion, which he called Woodlands Castle, during the years between 1800 and 1820. And, as we have seen, Henry Lucas had his pleasant little mansion in the Uplands.

I last mentioned Henry's eldest daughter Caroline Catherine, known as Cathy or Caroline, living with her father and stepmother at Uplands Villa in the 1840s. Despite the rift between them, Henry had seen to it that his elder children received a good education. By the time Caroline had finished her schooling she was immensely well read with considerable knowledge of the classics and modern languages; and her tastes became increasingly literary and scientific. Her notebooks for the 1840s show her preoccupation with natural history. Turning the pages we find careful drawings of unexpected subjects; of limestone fossils; of the peritoneal fluid in nereid worms; of the cellular reticulation of a boletus fungus; of the stamens and seed vessels of *Pedicularis sylvatica;* of a grasshopper found 'on the nasturtions at Rhossili'. She was also a sociable young lady and swapped drawings of a more traditional kind with her friends. Her scrapbook of about 1840 has pencil sketches of Penrice Castle by Miss Talbot, classical heads by Mrs Traherne and Mrs Sparks, and ponies by her cousin Minnie. There are landscapes by Miss Benson, portraits by Miss Mavor and Mrs Edwards and a good sprinkling of gaily painted flowers and butterflies.

By the time she was 30 Caroline had become a regular contributor to *Chambers Journal,* no small achievement for a provincial young woman of those times. In the pages of this famous weekly magazine devoted to the arts and sciences, Caroline discoursed learnedly and elegantly on such subjects as owls, petrels, lichens, ferns, frogs, bats and toads; and reviewed books about the countryside. I wonder what her father and the vulgar stepmother thought of all this intellectual activity.

It was probably in 1848, when Caroline was 26, that her father left Swansea for good. The next eight years saw the growth of Caroline's friendship with Mrs Charlotte Berrington of Woodlands Castle and her sister-in-law Augusta Hall, later Lady Llanover, whose home was at Llanover, a village on the banks of the Usk a few miles east of Abergavenny. This formidable woman, who left such an enduring mark on the history of Welsh culture in the 19th century, became Caroline's life-long friend. She was born in 1802, the younger daughter of Benjamin Waddington of Ty Uchaf — the White House — Llanover, an Englishman from Nottingham who had purchased Ty Uchaf at the close of the 18th century. Augusta's mother was Georgina Port, a niece of the Mrs Delany who had been friend and patron of Fanny Burney at the Court of George III. In 1823 Augusta Waddington married Benjamin Hall, whose father, another Benjamin, was a partner and son-in-law of Richard Crawshay the founder of the great ironworks at Cyfarthfa. The younger Benjamin's principal claim to fame was as a politician. He became first Commissioner of Works in Lord Palmerston's Government in 1855 and it was under his aegis that the great clocktower at Westminster was erected, the clock being named 'Big Ben' after him. He was made Lord Llanover in 1859. The Halls lived at Llanover Park, 'a huge barrack in the Gothic style' designed by Thomas Hopper and built close to the old Waddington home Ty Uchaf.

Benjamin Hall had a sister Charlotte who, in 1827, had married

Jenkin Davies Berrington junior of Swansea. His father, J. D. Berrington senior, was a Swansea solicitor who counted the Lucases of Stouthall among his clients. We have seen that Woodlands Castle, which is now called Clyne Castle and is a Hall of Residence for the University College of Swansea, was the creation of General George Warde around 1820. When the General died in 1830 he was heavily in debt and Woodlands Castle had to be sold. Benjamin Hall as a family trustee bought the estate as a home for his sister and her husband. The Berringtons lived at Woodlands Castle until 1859. Charlotte was a woman of parts, translating and publishing a learned work by one Albert Schultz entitled *An Essay on the influence of Welsh tradition upon the literature of Germany, France and Scandinavia.* She was also a gifted painter and illustrator of botanical subjects, and it is easy to see how Caroline's friendship with the Berringtons and Halls must have developed. Caroline was already an enthusiast for the Welsh language and culture which seemed so sadly in decline. We may trace this back to her childhood at Taliaris in the heart of Welsh speaking Carmarthenshire. One remembers how her elder brother Loftus on a visit to Builth in the 1830s was 'quite in a rage because the people all seem to speak English'.

Lady Llanover was the centre, the wellspring, of the Celtic revival of the 1840s. To this Englishwoman living in Monmouth-shire, Welsh became an obsession. As a young woman she was strongly influenced by the work and teaching of the Reverend Thomas Price of Crickhowell, an historian and antiquary and ardent advocate of the cause of his native tongue and traditions. She adopted a Bardic pseudonym 'The Bee of Gwent' and although in reality she spoke but little Welsh she organised her household on what she considered to be Welsh lines, and gave Welsh titles to her servants. It is not surprising that Lady Llanover was often laughed at by her contemporaries for her sometimes uncritical enthusiasms and 'Celtic' absurdities, and for her attempt to introduce Welsh-speaking families, complete with bearded Welsh pastor, into this very English part of Monmouthshire as it then was. But no doubt Caroline found Llanover much to her taste. The housemaids were dressed in old-fashioned white 'crossovers'. Dinner was at two, announced gravely in Welsh by Dan the butler, and during the meal Welsh airs were played by Griffith the family harper, a splendid figure in a scarlet and white check double-breasted coat, knee breeches, white stockings, and shoes with silver buckles. Griffith was a celebrated player of the old triple stringed Welsh harp – a difficult instrument to play as instead of having pedals to put a single row of strings into different keys, each tone and half-tone had its own string. High tea was taken at eight in the dining room after which, so it was said, Lady Llanover collected the unused lumps of sugar and emptied them with a great clatter into a box, which she locked. The day ended with the company kneeling on the cold flagstones of the servants' hall for what one visitor described as 'long-winded Methodistical prayers'. On Sundays the more conventional guests accompanied Lord Llanover to morning service in the village church, while in the afternoon Lady Llanover attended Chapel 'in strict Welsh dress — pointed tall hat with feather and close frilled cap under it, scarlet mantle fur bordered, and a shortish skirt'.

For all her eccentricities Lady Llanover was excellent company and an entertaining conversationalist who had the gift of gathering interesting people into her circle. She was a great patron and benefactor of the arts in Wales and helped to preserve many valuable manuscripts for the nation. She was also an excellent writer — witness her medley on Welsh cookery entitled *The Hermit of the Cell of St Gover,* and her scholarly edition of *The Autobiography and Correspondence of Mrs Delany* which she published in six volumes in 1861. She was said to be a bigoted Protestant although her only daughter and heiress became the wife of Arthur Herbert the Roman Catholic squire of Llanarth.

Lady Llanover was a matchmaker, although not always with success. She was particularly anxious to arrange a marriage for her husband's nephew, Constance Berrington's son Arthur. This young man became a great favourite with Lord Llanover who employed him as his secretary and confidante, and contemplated making him his heir, having no son of his own. In furtherance of this design Arthur, already a widower, was to be found a fresh wife and a seat in Parliament. Not only was Lord Llanover unsuccessful in persuading the young man to enter politics but worse still Arthur steadfastly refused to marry the girl whom Lady Llanover had found for him. This was Betha Johnes the younger daughter and co-heiress of Judge John Johnes of Dolaucothi whose family was, as we saw in an earlier chapter, connected with the Lucases by marriage. Lady Llanover's plan ended in disaster, with Betha desperately in love with Arthur, and Arthur quite determined not to have her. Lady Llanover's fury was unbounded, her pen vitriolic. 'That most dreadful being' she wrote of Arthur, 'scarcely thinking him human'.

Lady Llanover's matchmaking did not always end in failure. In the autumn of 1856 a letter of more than usual interest was delivered to the Rev J. P. Lucas at Rhosili.

> Llanover, Abergavenny
> Sept 28 1856
>
> Reverend Sir,
>   Although we have never met I am sure the announcement I have to make will not be considered out of place from my hand — Your excellent sister has accepted the proposal of that eminent man Sir Gardner Wilkinson, who has been here on a visit for some time. She will of course write herself — but as this has taken place under my roof I cannot refrain from saying that I think her *most fortunate*. Sir Gardner is *not a rich man* and therefore his attachment is more disinterested. He is, as you know, of *more* than *European* celebrity and is as much esteemed in private life as he is admired for his literary talents and his Antiquarian knowledge.
>   He begs me to say all that is proper on his part — and I beg to add that if you should be coming this way when they are here I hope to have the pleasure of seeing you.
>   I am, Reverend Sir,
>   Yours sincerely
>   Aug Hall
> Sir Benj: is from home, or would write in compts.

Caroline and Sir Gardner were married in the ancient church of Llanover beside the River Usk on the 16th October 1856. He was fifty-nine and she was thirty-four. They had no children but their marriage was an extremely happy one. Sir Gardner Wilkinson (1797–1875) was a man of prodigious learning, perhaps the greatest living authority on the civilisations of Ancient Egypt. Educated at Harrow and Oxford, he went abroad as a young man to Italy intending to study fortification before entering the army, but he soon became fascinated with the study of antiquity and resolved to devote himself to archaeology in Egypt. Here he spent the next twelve years, studying and drawing monuments, opening tombs and making maps.

In 1837 he published a three-volume work *The Manners and Customs of the Ancient Egyptians* which earned him a knighthood and the acclaim of scholars throughout Europe and America. Less well known are Sir Gardner's delightful and sympathetic watercolours and sketches of contemporary village life in Egypt, now in the British Museum. Before his marriage in 1856 Sir Gardner also travelled widely in the Levant and eastern Europe, and made a special study of Greek vases and Etruscan antiquities.

Sir Gardner was, with all his learning, a friendly and affable man 'of a bright and joyous nature' as his wife wrote of him. We have a glimpse of him during his time in Egypt from a letter written in 1831 by the young Disraeli, then touring the near East, to his sister Sarah:

> We were a week at Thebes with the advantage of the
> society of Mr Wilkinson, an Englishman of vast learning
> who has devoted years to the study of hieroglyphics and
> Egyptian antiquities, and who can read you the side of an
> obelisk or the front of a pylon as we would the last number
> of the *Quarterly*.

It was not only visiting Europeans who were impressed by this earnest scholar riding on horseback under the burning desert sun, sketching, noting and transcribing. He was much loved by the desert Arabs and the poor people of Thebes among whom he lived, and it was said that after his final departure from Egypt his apartments were kept swept and clean for twenty years by his servants hoping that he would some day return.

After their marriage Caroline lost no time in introducing her husband to Gower. The first visit to Rhosili was a success. Sir Gardner and the Rector took to each other and soon became close friends. Sir Gardner busied himself planting lilac trees in the Rectory garden and no doubt talked gardening with Aunt Harriet for whom he had brought some cyclamen plants. After the visit he wrote cheerfully to the Rector wishing him 'many happy returns of snow and mince pies'. For a time the Wilkinsons lived in Portman Square in London where they passed a sociable existence with many friends. Sir Gardner would do all his work in the drawing room, sometimes returning late in the evening from a party and then settling down to work through the night until six in the morning. During the day he would work steadily in the drawing room, pausing to receive friends and callers and then turning happily back to his papers.

Caroline too had been very busy with her writing. Shortly before her marriage she had published a treatise on the early church entitled *The Church of England Not Descended from the Church of Rome* — a theme no doubt warmly applauded by Lady Llanover — which displays Caroline's erudition and research into the abstruse depths of ecclesiastical history in the dark ages. Now, in the early years of her marriage, she was able to complete another work which was published in 1858 under the title *Weeds and Wildflowers*. This consists of over fifty essays on British Wildflowers, illustrated by woodcuts and some fine hand-painted engravings by Charlotte Berrington. Caroline's book is very unlike a modern flora. Etymology is discussed at length and historical and literary references to the plant are quoted in considerable detail. The description of the plants is precise, and the extent of her literary research may be judged from the fact that, to take one example, she lists for the plant Agrimony in addition to its formal Latin classification, ten different Welsh names — how pleasing to Lady Llanover! — and its common names in French, German, Dutch, Spanish, Russian and Japanese.

The book was published at the price of half a guinea by a Mr Van Voorst, a leading publisher of popular books on natural history. He also bought the copyright for £25 and six author's copies. The book was well received. One enthusiast ordered 120 reprints of the chapter on the Nettle at twopence each. 'I think you told me that the Nettle was your favourite weed' wrote Mr Van Voorst rather fatuously to the authoress. 'No, I *never* said such a thing!' was Caroline's indignant comment. There were some favourable reviews. 'Botany,' commented one, 'when pursued by a cultivated mind in this way becomes a guide to very extensive reading and we hardly know one who has done more to illustrate it than this accomplished writer.' Another reviewer thought the book 'particularly suitable for ladies . . . No intellectual pursuit is more innocent in itself or better fitted to preserve a healthful tone in the youthful mind and guard against the frivolities of gay society. We wish' he added 'that such refreshing and elevating studies were introduced also amongst the working classes as a safeguard against the low tastes and pursuits which beset a town life.'

Sir Gardner's health had been precarious since his days in Egypt, and by the early 1860s he was advised to curtail his literary work and take life more easily. In the autumn of 1863 Caroline too was taken ill; and in December she and Sir Gardner embarked at Southampton on the P&O Company steamer *Ceylon* of 1500 tons for a voyage to Gibraltar and Spain, in search of health. The sea was calm but Caroline remained in her berth throughout the four-day voyage to Gibraltar where they transferred to another ship the *Britannia* which was moored in the harbour. 'I being hoisted from the yard arm in a chair and wrapped in a union jack — as I was so lame', wrote Caroline. By Christmas they were in Cadiz, a visit which prompted a letter from an old friend Captain Ross RN, writing from Llanover.

Tue 19th January [1864]

My dear Lady Wilkinson,

I am left in charge of your sister and Miss Bonville till tomorrow when I return to Llanelly — having finished Tea I cannot do better, I hope, than to congratulate you and Sir Gardner upon your delightful change of climate which no doubt is already much benefitting you. On Saturday evening I came here and then heard of your flight to Cadiz; when in Church the following day the greater part of the time was occupied in thinking on the past, and on the last time I saw that Port. It was also on a beautiful Sunday about three weeks or less before the Battle of Trafalgar, Lord Nelson having ordered us to go as close as possible into Cadiz and most carefully reconnoitre the combined fleets of France and Spain then lying in the harbour.

So off the dear Frigate started, leaving the fleet outsight of land — fine light breeze from the north — till we, using a sailor's expression, could nearly throw a biscuit on the Ramparts. Our officers were all in the Tops laying down with their glasses carefully reporting to others the state and condition of every one of the Enemy's ships — as soon as the helm was put up and yards squared, I should say braced by — running parallel to the shore. The Ramparts were covered with spectators. We fancied we heard their voices. To our surprise not a gun was fired at us, in place of getting as we expected, and deserved, a good hammering.

Our work being done in a most satisfactory manner we returned to the fleet, and were then sent off to Algiers with presents to the Day of Algiers, who behaved so insolently as to cause us not to deliver them. Up anchor, to return in hopes to be in time for the battle. But when half way to Gibraltar, on a Sunday, a man of war Brig the Halcyon hove in sight and telegraphed 'We have gained the Victory but lost Nelson'. When made known to us, the dismay and sorrow throughout the Frigate was indescribable — no joy was shown on account of the Victory.

I am sure you and Sir Gardner will be tired with this yarn — therefore Goodnight and with kindest regards to Sir Gardner and sincerely best wishes to yourself believe me my dear Lady Wilkinson

Ever most sincerely and gratefully obliged

C. H. Ross

The Wilkinsons stayed in Spain until the spring — at Cadiz and nearby Puerto de Santa Maria. Caroline was delighted by the unfamiliar sights and sounds, the architecture, the costumes, the carnivals, the children playing on bladders which sounded like 'a multitude of new born babies crying' — but above all by the wild flowers — and her health improved steadily. She was unable to get about much, but Sir Gardner would go for walks and bring back bunches of flowers from the roadside and hedgerows, which he and Caroline would identify together. Sir Gardner like his wife was a keen botanist, and it was a sorrow to both of them that he was never able to publish his *Plants of the Eastern Desert of Egypt* which, so Caroline tells us, contains drawings 'of unrivalled delicacy and fidelity'.

On their return to England what must have seemed a heaven-sent opportunity occurred for them to go to live in Gower which they both loved. Brynfield House in Reynoldston had been, as we saw in an earlier chapter, Colonel Lucas's home since his daughter Minnie married Colonel Wood in 1843. Now Colonel Lucas had died, his widow had gone to live with her stepdaughter at Stouthall, and Brynfield was vacant. The Wilkinsons took a lease of the house from the Stouthall estate, and settled happily in Reynoldston. They made considerable alterations and additions to Brynfield, including, it is said, a room with specially heightened ceiling to accommodate an Egyptian mummy. While Sir Gardner studied the local antiquities or worked at his papers in the library with his old dog snoozing on the hearthrug beside him, Caroline was busy with her sketch book on Cefn Bryn and the Rhosili cliffs and round about the Gower villages. Although her skill with brush and pencil was in no way exceptional she has left us an interesting record of Gower churches, farms and cottages as they were in the mid 19th century, and some pleasant sepia landscapes. She was accurate in her work and interested in architectural detail. Natural history was not neglected and Caroline's *Book of Crabs* contains about fifty life-size paintings of crabs found at Rhosili and elsewhere.

Brynfield, the home at Reynoldston to which the Wilkinsons became so much attached, is built on an ancient dwelling site which seems to have formed part of the Lucas property since Tudor times. Near the house is a round enclosure about 50 yards in diameter, defended by a bank and external ditch. Pottery thought to be Roman has been found in this ditch. The name Brynfield was given to the house which, as we have seen, was built in about 1800 by the

Rev James Edwards, and may have incorporated part of the older Shepherd's Lodge. The Rev J. D. Davies recounts the story of the old house in an article in the Gower Church Magazine for September 1902 with his customary and delightful blend of legend, fact and reminiscence:

> It is said that the apparition of a lady dressed in white used frequently to be seen by the old people on the high road near Brynfield House; and sometimes she was seen sitting on the stone stile which was formerly alongside the churchyard gate . . . Before the late Sir Gardner Wilkinson improved and enlarged it, it was a good house bearing indications of having originally been a building of considerable size, parts of which had been pulled down. There used to be an ivy covered wall projecting westward from the main building, with a blocked up aperture of what appeared to have been originally a window of large size. When Sir Gardner was renovating the old house he removed some earth and rubbish at the base of the wall and in doing so he came across some fragments of beautiful painted glass. Upon one of the broken pieces the letters E R could be made out very distinctly. The evidence of this window and the painted glass with which it was formerly filled shows that the house must once upon a time have been a residence of consequence, and inhabited by people of note.
>
> Lady Wilkinson was of the opinion that it was originally a religious house inhabited by a sisterhood of the order of St Clare, called from their poverty the 'poor Clares' alias the 'poor Ladies' whose habit was grey. Furthermore she informed me that the two cottages adjoining the churchyard, lately built (sic) by her brother the Rev J. Ponsonby Lucas, stand on the site of an old thatched house which went by the curious name of the Maiden's Fancy, and in some old deeds which she had seen is called the White Ladies, and that the ancient well which is close by, used to be called the White Ladies well. It is still known as the Ladies' well. The account of the apparition probably grew out of this sisterhood of St Clare, whose grey habit was doubtless often to be seen in the neighbourhood in pre-reformation days. I do not know whether any documentary evidence exists bearing upon the foundation of a religious community of the poor Clares at Reynoldston but from what I have been able to put together as above, it appears not unlikely. The disappearance of the community would date back to the suppression of all the monasteries and religious houses in the time of Henry VIII. The story is not devoid of interest although it lacks the confirmation of historical proof.

I still have the pieces of glass which Sir Gardner found at Brynfield. When my father took them to the British Museum in 1936 they were dated to the early part of the 15th century, so the evidence for an important house on this site in medieval times does seem to be strong.

Throughout her married life Caroline was an ardent collector of recipes. Her old black exercise book bulges with a remarkable collection of dishes culled from her many friends and relations in south and mid Wales. We can try Dolaucothi potato pudding, Aunt Harriet's tart paste, Aunt Sibthorp's pigs head collared, or Mrs Pritchard of Usk's method of cooking crimped salmon. For adventurous cooks there is Lady Llanover's complicated but untried recipe for raw chicken fricasseed, and if this fails we can fall back on 'Lord Llanover's pudding'. For coughs and colds there is a choice of Mrs Edwards of Gileston's liquorice tea, or Mrs Herbert of Llanarth's Italian cook's recipe for pearl barley and lettuce water; or we can try a wine-glass of 'coal milk' from a recipe which begins 'Take some nice lumps of common coal'. Butlers and housekeepers were consulted through the post on domestic problems, and happily disclosed to Caroline their professional expertise: 'My lady, I beg leave to say to make French Polish dissolve 2 ozs of gum shellac in ½ pint of spirits of wine . . .' 'Honoured Lady Wilkinson I will with pleasure give your Ladyship directions to wash flannel . . .'

During the 1870s the Wilkinsons suffered increasingly from ill health. In October 1875 while on a visit to Caroline's sister Maria Sir Gardner was taken ill and died a few days later. He had appointed the Rev J. P. Lucas as executor, so Caroline and her brother were left with the task of sorting through his papers and collections which were left to be divided between Harrow School and the British Museum. There was little money for the support of his widow. Caroline's plight was brought to the notice of Disraeli. The Prime Minister had not forgotten the man who had showed him round ancient Thebes more than 40 years ago, and found time to persuade Queen Victoria to grant Caroline a modest pension in recognition of her husband's services to science and archaeological literature.

Caroline gave up Brynfield and went to live at Bank House, Llandovery, where for a few years she was able to busy herself with the preparation of a new edition of *The Manners and Customs of the Ancient Egyptians*. This was published in 1878 under the

Rhosili Church in 1855. The day before the restoration began, from a drawing by Caroline Lucas.

editorship of a friend of Sir Gardner's at the British Museum. Caroline included a dedication to Disraeli — Lord Beaconsfield as he had by then become — and Queen Victoria was graciously pleased to accept a copy of the work in two volumes for the Royal Library at Windsor Castle. The Queen showed her gratitude for the gift, perhaps predictably, by presenting Caroline with Sir Theodore Martin's *Life of the Prince Consort*, in five volumes.

Caroline died in October 1881. The letters of condolence which poured in to Rhosili Rectory show a more than conventional sorrow. Darling Cathy had been greatly loved by her friends. 'Words cannot fully express my feelings on this most grievous event', wrote Lady Llanover to the Rector, 'grievous to you and to those little boys beyond all others, but to her old old friends and to myself her place can never be filled. Her tastes and interests in life have been interwoven with my own.'

The 'little boys' referred to by Lady Llanover were the Rector's sons. Why she mentioned them so particularly in her letter will appear in the next chapter.

7

1870–89
Life at Rhosili Rectory

The Rector and his wife had eight children — nine if you count an infant son who only lived for a few hours. I list them below with their full names; those grand sounding names which seem to accentuate the social isolation of the family living in this remote Gower Rectory down by the sea. The names reflect, of course, the Rector's peculiar pride in his aristocratic Irish connections; a pride which caused the long line of Johns to skip a generation; although Rebecca made a private note that the little boy who died at birth would always be John to her.

Charles Gardner Tottenham (Charles)	Caroline Tottenham (Caroline)
Louisa Loftus	Maria Louisa Loftus (May)
Loftus Tottenham (Loftus)	Henry Loftus Tottenham
Ponsonby Tottenham (Tottenham)	Flora Loftus Tottenham (Flora)

Of the six who survived infancy, Caroline died in her late 50s, Loftus, Tottenham and Flora in their 80s, and Charles and May lived to be over 90. Only Charles and Loftus married, and only Loftus had children. Charles being seven years older than any of the others was rather set apart from them in childhood. He was a steady hard working fellow, cautious, unadventurous, and of a disarming simplicity of character. At the age of 9 he was sent as a boarder to Cowbridge Grammar School, an ancient foundation where some of the South Wales gentry sent their sons if they could not afford the fees of an English Public School. Here life must have been pretty tough for a little boy, but Charles was not one to complain. I quote some of his letters home, written in 1869 when he was 10 years old, starting his second term at school:

My dear Papa,

How nice making the cat soup. I am glad you have cut the seagull's wing. Does it peck itself now? In which feild is Daisy now in? I am so very glad that the kitten is safe. Can it run about yet? The plum tart must have seemed very nice coming from our own garden. Tell dear little Ba [Loftus] that I am always thinking of him. I bathed today. I am trying dear Papa to do my lessons well. I sleep in my own little corner still and Phillips sleeps with me but is a little more merciful. I have bought a nice little 6d prayer book, and above all I have actually had my photagrahph taken for 6d. I cannot send it you for it is done in glass and has a little gilt frame.

I am ever Dear Papa your very loving son
    C. G. T. Lucas

My dear Mama

I was very tired on Wednesday night and to finish off I got a crumb against my tooth at tea which gave me a bad tooth ache for the rest of the evening. The mystery I want you to rissolve is wether the Blackbird liked being shot as well as eating goose berries. Dear little baby was very loving and I only wish I had shown more inclination to play with him when I was at home. The fish must have been much in the seagul's line. I know how I was missed. In one corner of the pew I stuck one of Papa's little tooth picks and there I hope it will remain.

I am now going to tell you a full account of the managerie which I went to yesterday evening. First of all I started from here to go to the milfield. In here I found this grand menagerie and crowds of peaple of all ages and classes all pressing to pay their shilling and get a ticket. At last after pushing boys down and tearing mens coats and receiving a great deal of cursing and swering in return I got in and the first I saw was 3 great camels. I was told they were not savage so I played a long time with them and gave them bread. Then I walked on an saw 1 polar Bear very savage, 4 royal Bengal tigers v.s. 5 enormous lions v.s. 2 wolves v.s. 3 jackals v.s. Next 4 enormous elepthants which the man (to my great delight) said 'Emporor' said he 'open the gate and come out'. And the Elephant with his trunk opened the gate and came out. Then he told the Elephant to give us a song, and he went er er er er gah. Now we'll have a steeple chase, said he, so 2 men came forward and one said he'd ride Betsy and the other Emporor, so they were dressed up like Punch and Judy and a gate was put up in the middle and the elepants jumped over it. Then they went back to their den and I put a peny in Emporor's trunk and he put it in a little box. I then bought a great many apples nuts and biscutis for the monkeys elephants and camels. I have not told ½ my story but cannot finish it now. I write on this paper because a sheet of slave paper would not hold it.

I am Dear Mama your loving son
  CGTL

September 3rd
Cowbridge

My Dear Mama,

I do not mean that Phillips sleeps in the same bed with me. Have you received the mark list? I suppose the kitten is quite a big cat now. The seagull is no doubt now quite tame. How is dear little Ba? It is now a case of a game of marbles so good bye dear Mama.

I am ever your very loving son
  CGTL

In later life Charles became very set in his habits. During some 60 years as a London solicitor it was said that he invariably ate his frugal lunch at the same Lyons tea shop at the corner of the Strand and Essex Street and always took the same fortnight's holiday each year at the same lodgings at Hove or Worthing, I forget which.

The next son Loftus, my father, was much the most vigorous and enterprising of the children, always ready to take up a challenge and try something new. He was the natural leader in the children's activities, just as in later life his was the most potent voice in family plans and decisions. Like Charles he was unmusical, though he loved poetry for which he had a good ear. He could write passable verse, draw accurately and meticulously, and wrote a very good letter. He had a gift for acting and mimicry, which he seldom exercised. From an early age, with his great charm and courtesy of manner, he was adept not only at doing things for other people, but at getting others to do things for themselves. During his many years of command at sea, in a variety of ships and with seamen of all races, he never had trouble with officers or crew. He was intensely loyal, and unyielding in his judgment of men and affairs. Mother once said to me about him: 'Dad sees everything either black or white, where you and I like to see things grey.'

Tottenham had a deeply reserved nature. As a boy and throughout life he seemed unable to achieve a real personal relationship. He drew back from life. On the surface he was easy enough, loved cricket and tennis and sea bathing, yet his conversation — or so it seemed to his nephews and nieces — was empty and banal. Tottenham could only express himself through music. When he left Llandovery school with an Exhibition in classics to Oriel College Oxford his headmaster said he was the best musician the school had produced in 40 years. When he first started at boarding school as a little boy of nine there were few tears so far as anyone could observe. Several days after he left home his mother lifted the lid of the family piano to find, lying across the keys, a piece of paper on which was written in a childish hand the single word 'Goodbye'.

Caroline — she was known as Croll — is to me rather a shadowy figure, dogged by ill health and confined to the daily domestic round. May and Flora were dears. They had sweet and tunable voices and played well on the piano. May was the pretty one,

The old Rectory, Rhosili,

bookish rather, and apt to be critical. Flora, whose plainness was accentuated in childhood by her hair brushed hard back from her forehead and an impossible pair of pince-nez perched on her nose, was the warmer of the two. She too loved books and poetry and spent most of her life teaching the children of her family and relations the three Rs and good manners. On the subject of table manners she started early. As a little girl of three, standing on a box and leaning over the door of the pigsty she was heard to remark, in a reproving tone 'Take a 'poon, pig.'

Two attributes which I have not so far mentioned were common to the whole family. One was their love for their home. The remote and beautiful situation of Rhosili Rectory seems to have had a profound effect on them all. From the Rector down they loved every stick and stone of the place, and relished the lights and colours of the Gower landscape and the changing patterns of weather, wind and tide. They were an intensely close knit family, and if they had any criticisms of each other these were subjects which, like sex and money, they never mentioned in public. They had the quaint but charming habit of always referring to each other, both in talking and writing, as Dear Mother, Dear Flora, Dear Loftus, etc, and somehow they really meant it. They shared an old-fashioned courtesy, with some little tricks of speech from an earlier age — a bookcase was a 'bookas' and a vase was a 'vawse'. Above all they shared laughter, and a rich enjoyment of anyone and anything that seemed to them pompous or absurd.

The girls were sent as boarders to Carmarthen High School. Loftus and Tottenham went not to Cowbridge Grammar School as might have been expected but to Llandovery. In 1847 a new school had been founded at Llandovery, endowed by a wealthy benefactor; at a time when, according to a contemporary, 'The education of the young is lamentably neglected in Wales and there has not been for many years a school of any celebrity or merit in any part of it.' The object of the benefactor Thomas Phillips was to provide a sound liberal education and — what was uppermost in the founder's mind — a knowledge of the Welsh language and culture. The trust deed stipulated that Welsh must be taught exclusively during one hour of every school day and during that period Welsh should be the sole means of communication throughout the school. The Welsh language was to be 'at all times religiously and faithfully observed as the primary and chief intent and object of the Institution'.

Thomas Phillips was in his eighties, and lived in London, and he left the setting up of the school to others. It will come as no surprise that the driving force behind the foundation was Augusta Hall, Lady Llanover. She was a trustee of the school from its foundation in August 1847 until her death over 50 years later. She donated the land on which the school was built and over the years devoted much time, effort and money to its advancement. She took particular pleasure in donating annual prizes for excellence in the Welsh language. Between 1847 and 1900 the school had seven Wardens, all clergymen of high scholastic and educational attainments. The assistant masters were almost invariably Oxford or Cambridge graduates, many with first class degrees. The effect of all this talent was not, however, quite what Lady Llanover and her co-trustees expected and hoped for. Llandovery became more and more of an English Public School and less and less of a Welsh Collegiate Institution.

The last of the 19th century Wardens to show much interest in the Welsh language was the Rev William Watkins MA appointed Warden in 1861 at the age of 25. He was an old boy of the school, a mathematician — 13th wrangler at Cambridge — and had for a few years been assistant master at Eton. His wife was Maria one of the daughters of Henry Lucas IV. Watkins was a fine scholar and an inspiring teacher and during his 14 years as Warden the school won many scholarships to Oxford and Cambridge. Mathematical awards at Cambridge predominated, reflecting the Warden's skill as a teacher. But unfortunately Watkins, though strong on scholarship, was weak on organisation and discipline. There was not, as yet, a thorough going boarding house system. Boys were lodged about in the town and tended to spend their evenings not in the pursuit of learning but smoking in public houses. The reputation of the school suffered and numbers dropped as low as 40.

In 1875 Watkins was succeeded as Warden by the second master the Rev Dr A. G. Edwards. He proved to be a headmaster of great ability and during his ten years as Warden the school became known as 'the premier school in Wales', reaching a standard of excellence both academically and at Rugby football which rivalled the best of the English Public Schools. Loftus and Tottenham were fortunate that their schooldays were spent under a headmaster of such high calibre. Loftus joined the school in 1876 at the age of 9, and Tottenham a few years later.

It must be admitted that Dr Edwards had no time at all for the

Welsh language and under his regime Welsh became an optional subject and the terms of the trust deed were blatantly ignored. So too were the annual prizes awarded by Lady Llanover. It was her custom to prepare, with the aid of distinguished Welsh scholars, the annual examination papers in Welsh and send them to the Warden. In 1879 Edwards received the papers but omitted to organise the competition. The following year, mindful no doubt of Lady Llanover's severe displeasure at this dreadful lapse, he did go so far as to organise the competition, but entirely forgot to inform her of the result or ask her for the prizes. Months later one boy plucked up courage to write to her Ladyship informing her that he had won the prize for translating Andromache's speech to Hector from Greek into Welsh and asking for his prize money which was £2–10–0. Lady Llanover's anger with the Warden was such that she decided to ignore him altogether and wrote an icy letter to the Western Mail as senior trustee of the school, laying bare his misdeeds and inviting the other seven winners to get in touch with her.

In December 1877 Loftus, then aged 11, was in quarantine for some childish complaint and unable to go home at the end of term. It was arranged that he should spend Christmas at Llanover where his aunt Lady Wilkinson would also be staying. Lady Llanover wrote to his parents:

> Dec 21st 1877
> Lady Llanover presents her compliments to Mr and Mrs Lucas and hopes that they will oblige her by allowing their excellent and well conducted little son Loftus to remain in her care when Lady Wilkinson is obliged to go to London, and to be joined at Llanover by his elder and younger brother to remain there from the end of this month till the school opens at Llandovery, when the boys could go much quicker and more directly without stoppages than if they returned to Rhosili first. From the specimen of the family who Lady Llanover has now the pleasure of seeing she is very anxious to make acquaintance with his two brothers to whom her excellent friend Lady Wilkinson is so much attached — Little Loftus is *very well* and *very happy* and keeps early hours. He seems to be quite at home tho' in *good order* and will be able to shew his brothers everything.

The Rector and his wife were no doubt very pleased that Loftus had been such a success with his formidable hostess, but they knew that he would be determined to come home for at least part of the holidays, and so it was arranged.

Llanover Dec 28. 1877
Friday night

Lady Llanover presents her compliments to the Reverend
Ponsonby and Mrs Lucas and will really be much relieved
to hear that their *good* little boys arrived safe and without
being ill after such a very *seriously* long journey. Lady
Llanover feels quite uncomfortable about them as she
believes they will *not* get to the end of their journey till
eleven o'clock at night, and have a mile and a half after
they leave the omnibus before they reach home. She only
hopes that two *strong men* will meet them and carry them
home on their backs, well wrapt up. She has sent very
wholesome *chicken* sandwiches for the two youngest as
nothing is more indigestible than the diet in the railway
refreshment rooms. They have also biscuits and oranges
and cold tea and spring water and very light wholesome
buns, made in the morning, so that they can make their
dinner in the *train* and their tea and a *little* supper *also* and
Lady Llanover trusts that they will be allowed to sleep the
whole of the next day if so disposed without being called.

Lady Llanover has been much pleased with them. They
have been *very good* and their elder brother's care of them
is really admirable and Lady Llanover hopes that she may
see them all three again at some future opportunity. She
need not say that Lady Wilkinson never forgets them and
that they are indeed very happy in having such an aunt!
Lady Llanover hopes to hear of their perfect recovery after
the fatigues of this journey.

The fatigues of the journey were of course nothing as compared
with the excitement of coming home, and if Lady Llanover
thought that two schoolboys would submit to being carried home
on the backs of two strong men she must have been considerably
out of touch! A typical home-coming from Llandovery for the
Christmas holidays was remembered by Loftus. The Rector had
come into town on business and met the boys at Swansea High
Street station. Then followed the excitement of shopping, the two
boys in tam o'shanter caps and the Rector in frock coat and top
hat. In Oxford Street they boarded the two-horse omnibus for
Rhosili, the boxes were hoisted on to the roof, old Button the
driver climbed to his seat and lit his pipe, and they were off on
their 18-mile journey through the gathering dusk of the winter
afternoon. The bus journey ended at Pitton Cross and a waggon
took aboard the few passengers for Rhosili. Here Charles and
John Richards the Parish Clerk were waiting at the Green. The
boys' boxes were left to be collected next day, and in the winter

darkness, greeted by the salt sea wind and the welcoming roar of the surf, a little procession started along the path to the Rectory. The Rector led the way carrying a lantern and calling out a warning 'Pool!' from time to time. Next came Charles carrying wraps, then the two boys, and at a slight but respectful distance from the family party John Richards brought up the rear with the smaller baggage slung across his back. The evening ended with the boys and their parents — the girls were in bed — seated round the dining room table enjoying a late feast of roast pork.

The Rhosili omnibus 1880, bringing the boys home from school, from a drawing by Loftus Lucas.

During the Christmas holiday of 1883/4 Loftus kept a diary in an exercise book. I have transcribed it as it was written. He was then just 17, having left Llandovery and joined the school ship Conway as a sea cadet — of which more later. Tottenham was 14, Caroline 12, May 11 and Flora 6. Charles at 24 seems to have been away from home throughout the holiday. The Helme family referred to in the diary lived at Hillend on the north side of Rhosili Down. Sheepen Park was the field where the Rector kept his sheep penned in the winter. Tom is Tom Richards of Keenmoor who helped the Rector with his farming and Ann is the maid at the Rectory. Diles is the lake (Gower word for stream) which flows out onto Rhosili bay north of the Down, and Rolling Taw (tor) is the bluff on the south west corner of the Down. The Rocket House, beside the Rectory path near the village, housed the rocket apparatus which was used to fire a line to ships wrecked near the shore.

Friday 21st [December] – First day of the holidays, after breakfast went up to Clerk's house with old barrow and brought down my chest, went straight back again and brought down Croll's box and a parcel of grocery, then I went back again bringing down both Tott's boxes, the (Mrs Helme's) cake and two wraps. Tott accompanied me in the first load, and the girls and Tott (who brought down four wraps) in the 3rd load. Afterwards went to 'Sheepen-Park' with Father. After dinner helped Mother to unpack my chest, etc, after tea read Longman's Magazine.
PS – I may say that after bringing down those three heavy loads, the old wheelbarrow was as strong as before she started. Heard that seven of Beynon of Sluxon's sheep, two of Powell's, and two of somebody else's, had been killed by a dog in the night.

Saturday 22nd – Got up at 6 am and went (over the hill) to Keenmoor, asked Tom to lend me one of his donkeys, and after a good search found them strayed down to Middleton, bridled one and got home in time for breakfast. After breakfast started for Coity Green with donkey and 3 girls, to get evergreens for decorating the church, took the old wool-sack to prevent the holly pricking the donkey, got a splendid lot, had great difficulty in keeping the holly and ivy on the donkey's back, but got home in good time, gave the donkey a good feed, and had dinner. Afterwards got the holly etc up to the church and took the donkey on to Keenmoor, coming back over the hill. After tea (about ¼ past eight) started off to Pitton X to meet the omnibus. (Ann also went) and after waiting about there a good time the omnibus came, crowded as usual, got a parcel from D. C. Jones and arrived home about ¼ past ten. The weather was fine with a mild North Westerly wind. *Eight* more of Powell's sheep killed in the night.

Sunday 23rd – Went to church in the morning (Rhosili), after dinner stayed at home with Flora and read the Dawn of Day, ('dogs to die') and went with her up to the church to meet Mother, Tott and 2 girls. After tea had a Mariners' meeting, Father presided and read an account of a shipwreck and gallant rescue of the crew, the whole affair most droll.

Monday 24th – After breakfast went up to decorate the church, *soon* afterwards joined by Tott, after dinner came up again and was soon afterwards joined by Mother and two girls, and afterwards by Tott and Flora, the girls had worked with ivy leaves on brown paper, the words 'Glory to God', very nicely, and I put them up over the Chancel, they looked splendid, (I also hung a piece of holly in the porch.) Came home and picked some evergreens to put up in the house, which I did after tea. Heard that the dog had been fired at but not killed.

Tuesday 25th – Christmas day. Went to Rhossili church in the morning and when we came back heard that George Thomas had shot his thumb badly, so I ran up with some brandy for him and saw his thumb, it looked very bad, came back and had lunch, afterwards read etc and had dinner about four o'clock, which consisted of a beautiful turkey, boiled pork, plum pudding etc etc. Read a little after dinner, had crackers etc, tea, and went to bed.

Wednesday 26th – After breakfast went to the sands, and went up to the shop to change some money for Father, and to get some yeast. After dinner went again to the shop to get some bread with Mother, and on our way back called in to see how George Thomas was.

Thursday 27th – I was going to Port Eynon to get Father's coat which had gone there by mistake, and Father was going to see some people in Halfpenny Street etc etc so we started together, but in Middleton were caught up by Tott who told me that the coat had just been brought by a little girl (who came over the hill), so we all three went on together, first of all to Pitton X, then to Halfpenny Street to see poor William Richards who is very ill, of the same complaint that his poor sister died of, then to Mrs Bowen, then to Tom's house, then round Hawk's wall to see George Thomas, getting home in time for dinner. In the afternoon drew and painted, and practised the Charade. After tea drew and painted.

Friday 28th – Had a bad cold, did not go out much, cleared the wash house corner. After dinner sighted Sheepen Park. In the evening drew. (Practised Charade).

Saturday 29th – In the morning went to the sands. After dinner sighted Sheepen Park with Tott, etc, etc, after tea read, and then went up to Pitton X to meet omnibus, and brought down clock from Charles' lodgings, and a loaf of bread, Tott came with me and carried my lamp part of the way.

Sunday 30th – Went to church in the afternoon (Rhossili). To please Father I put on my best new uniform suit. Tott played. In the evening my tooth-ache came on.

Monday 31st – Bad tooth-ache. Tithe day. After breakfast went up to Pitton X, and brought down Charles' ship (which came on Saturday in omnibus). After dinner went to Mrs Rogers and George Thomas, and took Father's xmas box (2/6) to the clerk. (Put ghost up in thee etc etc)

Tuesday 1st Jan – Tooth-ache better. Father went to Llangennith, I stayed at home (my face being too much swollen to go with Father) and took the glass out of Charles' ship and cleaned it well, and mended a rope which had been broken. Sighted Sheepen Park after dinner. After tea drew.

Wednesday 2nd – After breakfast put up the ship in my room (over the window) with Mother. Afterwards went to George Thomas' house with some wadding. After tea drew.

Thursday 3rd – Went (after breakfast) up to Tom's house, with a letter from Mrs Helme, addressed under Father's care, I read it to them it was about the 'kitchen' also to the 'rich' Bevan's house to return an umbrella which she had lent to Mother. After dinner went to the sands with Father, Tott, Croll, Maria and Flora and walked to Diles. After tea read 'Jack's Courtship'.

Friday 4th – Went up to George Thomas'. After dinner went out with Father and Tott. After tea read.

Saturday 5th – A very wet morning, arranged my shells. After dinner went with Tott to get some eggs and got a few at Mrs Chalk's (Middleton). Tom came to clear out animals before tea. Afterwards at 8.30, went with Tott to meet omnibus, and brought down a grocery parcel, and a parcel of herrings in a basket the clerk lent me. Tott brought down another parcel.

Sunday 6th – All went to Rhossili church in the morning but Flora. I took the Holy Sacrament. Mother, in coming back, called to see George Thomas, found him pretty well. After lunch Mother, Tott, Croll and I went to the Sunday school, and to practise the singing, however, the weather being uncertain, none of the Llangennith singers came, and only four or five of our singers, but we practised till nearly four. Read in the evening.

Monday 7th – Got up at 6.30 am and went over the hill to Keenmoor, got one of Tom's donkeys which he lent me, and came home round the road in time for breakfast. After breakfast Tott and I started (with donkey) for Tom Grove's house to get some apples. When we got to his house, which we did with some difficulty, we had to go down to Tankeylake, as he kept his apples there. At last we started back with 2/- worth, (350) rather small but not bad. Got back just in time for dinner, (of course Tott did not ride at all on the donkey). After dinner went with Father to Barriston, to see the who was ill there. As Father had to go to the School Board meeting, I delayed taking back the donkey, to go up with him. We started at 6.30 and when we got to Middleton I went on to the shop to get 3d of yeast. I then took the donkey on to Tom's house, and came back again, waiting outside the school till Father came out, so we walked home together (got home at 9 pm). Had supper and wrote my diary.

Tuesday 8th – After breakfast did some navigation and then went out and cleared away a lot of dead stuff etc from the flower garden, had dinner and sighted Sheepen Park, went down to the sands and got a few shells etc, came back and walked about a little with Father. Came in and read till tea, after which I arranged my shells.

Wednesday 9th – After breakfast went up to Middleton to pay Mrs Chalk and Mrs Thomas for some eggs which I had got there, and to get a pint of milk at Beynons (the floored 'bus' man). Philip Thomas gave me a cocoanut, one of a good many which had come ashore under the sound (a vessel with that cargo having been wrecked in the channel). It was very nice and was full of milk. Tott came up to 'Rolling Taw' to meet me. After dinner sighted Sheepen Park and went down to the sands, found a few shells and came back, walked about a little with Father and came in and had a good practise at the Charade. After tea arranged my shells.

Thursday 10th – After breakfast went up to the church to get something for Mother which she had left there. Had dinner at 12 o'clock, directly after which Father, Mother, Tott and I started for Llanmadoc, to call on Mr Davies. It was a beautiful afternoon and we went straight over Llanm. hill, arriving at his house about 3. We had tea there after which he showed us his workshop which was beautiful. Then we started back again (over the hill). He came a little way with us. It was dark before we were off the Down (that

is to say we were walking by moonlight). Mother thought *nothing* of the walk. Well, we got home at 6.30, had tea, and rehearsed our charade.
PS – Nearly every night Tott and I perform some tricks.

Friday 11th – After breakfast did some navigation, then sighted Sheepen Park, came back and took the clerk's basket which he had lent me back. Tott came with me. Afterwards cleared the wash-house corner. After dinner went out a little, came in and had a good game. After tea Tott and I performed some tricks before Father, then we had a good rehearsal, did our scrap-books, and went to bed.
PS – At about 9pm Father and I go out to give the cow some hay.

Saturday 12th – After breakfast did some navigation, then sighted Sheepen Park, came back and found Tom here. He cleaned out the animals, and did some other odd jobs. Then we all went down to the sands, Tott and 2 girls remained to jump, and I took Flora on to the 'Cow and Calf'. After dinner Father and Mother went up to the village, and I went as far as the Rocket House with them. As they had different business to do they separated at Pitton, Father got home a long time before Mother, and I went to meet her as far as the Clerk's house. (I cleared the wash-house corner before I went to meet Mother). After tea we had a good rehearsal, then Tott and I started to meet the omnibus, it was a very bright moonlight night and as I knew Taylor's parcel was going to be a 'tidy weight', I took the new barrow up to the Rocket House. The omnibus came, very much crowded and very late, we got our parcels all right. Tott carried a loaf of bread and I carried Taylor's parcel to the Rocket House. We were very glad to find the barrow there. I brought home in it Taylor's parcel, and another basket which Ann brought down (she also went to Pitton X). We got back at 5 to 11, had baked potatoes for supper, and went to bed.
PS – The new barrow runs easier but is heavier on the arms than the old barrow.

Sunday 13th – Rhossili church in the afternoon. After breakfast Mother and the 2 girls went to the school, Father to Llangennith. I sighted Sheepen Park and came home by the sands, then Tott and I went up to meet Mother and the girls. After dinner all went to church, after which Father held the first Confirmation Class.

Monday 14th – After breakfast did some navigation. Went to see the sheep in Sheepen Park and noticed more than ever what a lot of bits of broken crockery and stones etc were lying about the field, so I fetched the old barrow and gathered as much as I could wheel, and threw it over the cliff. After dinner went up to the village with Mother, Croll, Maria and Flora. We went to the school and other places. Came back and had a rehearsal. After tea Mother, Tott and self started up to the school (it was the library night), there were a great many people there and Mother and the new schoolmistress sang 'home sweet home' and Tott played for them. We got away before 9. (Mother's voice completely drowned the schoolmistress').

Tuesday 15th – Got up and did some navigation before breakfast. Tom came to hedge. Went up to Beynon of Middleton to get a pint of milk. After dinner Mother went up to the village and I went up as far as George Thomas' house with her. Came back and remained with Tom. Went a little way to meet Mother, and had a rehearsal. After tea had another rehearsal.

Wednesday 16th – Dear Charles' birthday. In the morning I was occupied in putting the stage in order, and in the afternoon (when a cart of straw came) in putting up the curtains. At a few minutes past 8 pm the Act began. It went off splendidly, a first class reward for the time we had spent in getting it up. After it was finished Tott and I acted the 'Peep Show' (what is that yaller light?) They were all extremely pleased with this and Father said we were to act it every year. We then had baked potatoes for supper. (Father allowed Ann to see both Acts) after which (there being no wind and the night being so dark) Father let off the fireworks which had been in the house ever since Flora's birthday. Then I got and lit my bull's eye lamp, and Tott and I went half way up the path and in coming back set a furze bush on fire in honour of dear Charles' birthday.

Thursday 17th – After breakfast went to the sands with Tott, the girls came down afterwards. After dinner Father, Mother, Tott, Croll, Maria, Flora and self went to see Llangennith church, we all thought it most grand. After tea read 'Jack's Courtship' etc etc.

Friday 18th – After breakfast did some navigation. Afterwards went to the sands with Tott, and the three girls came down afterwards. After dinner went out with Tott and did different unimportant things. After tea read 'Jack's Courtship'.

Saturday 19th – Got up and had a cold bath before breakfast. After breakfast sighted Sheepen Park with Tott, and then went to the sands with him and had some jumps on the sand banks etc etc. After dinner went out and wheeled away the stalks of some cabbages, cleared the wash-house corner etc. After tea went up with Tott to meet the omnibus, a lot of parcels came and as the break was coming down to Rhossili we waited and put all the parcels in. We then ran on. When we got home I found I had dropped a little parcel (from Richards) containing a little bottle of oil of cloves (for tooth ache) so I went back after supper, nearly as far as the Ship, but could not find it. When I got home it was going on for one o'clock.

Sunday 20th – Rhossili church in the morning. After breakfast I went again to look for that parcel, all the others went to church. At the top of Pitton X hill I found the paper that had been torn off it with 'Revnd J. P. Lucas' on it, so I came back over the hill. When I was coming back it came on very wet, and I took some wraps and went to meet the others i.e. Father, Mother, Tott, Croll, Maria and Flora. They were very glad of them. After dinner I went with Mother to the Sunday School. (The others stayed at home and read).

Monday 21st – After breakfast went up to the shop to get some yeast, to Beynon to get a pint of milk, to the Cooper, to Rogers, and to the church to get a prayer book etc. After dinner Father, Croll, Maria, Tott and self started for the Red Chamber. It was agreed that we should meet Tom at 'Mewslade'! With Tom's help we everyone got down, Father and the two girls came as far as the opening of the passage, and then Tott and I proceeded alone with Tom. We went in to the very end and brought an old pitcher out, we broke off a quantity of beautiful crystal etc etc. Father gave Tom one shilling, also bought a rabbit which he caught then by putting his foot on it. We got back in good time for tea, after which we divided and labelled the crystal etc (kept two bits for Charles).

Tuesday 22nd – A very wet day. In the morning went up to Beynon's house to get some milk, and then read. After dinner sighted Sheepen Park. It was very wet. Afterwards played some games with Tott and the girls. After tea read 'Jack's Courtship' and cut some hay for the cow etc etc.

Wednesday 23rd – A very wet day. After breakfast did some navigation. Then made pegs — thus — for the covers of the 'maison' seats. About middle day a gale came on. After dinner went with Father and Tott to Llangennith to get eggs etc. After tea went up to Pitton X with a letter to order the break for Friday.

Thursday 24th – After breakfast Tott and I went up to get a donkey for the girls to ride. We went round Hawk's wall to Sarah Bevan's house and got their donkey and came home round the road. I then saddled him (side saddle) and took the three girls for a ride to the 'factory'. Flora rode as far as, or a little past the 'wet corner'. Then Maria rode on to the 'factory' (we stayed there some time to shelter from the rain). Then Flora rode back as far as the Hillend gate, and Croll rode all the way home. After dinner took the donkey back and got some sugar from the shop, also took one of Tott's pairs of boots to Bevan to have a few nails put in. About 4.30 started with Tott's white box (in new barrow) and landed it in the Clerk's house. Next I took up Croll's box and Tott pulled, and then I took Tott's other box up (it was dark by this time). After tea read etc.

Friday 25th – Tott and Croll went back to school. Started from the Clerk's house at about 9 am (all except Mother Maria and Flora) in break (one horse, 'Leicester') and got to Killay about 11.30, went by 11.49 train to Swansea. First went to Scott (dentist) then had some lunch at the Exchange Buildings. Tott and I went with Father and Croll to Landore. We saw Croll off and then all 3 returned to Swansea. Father did some other business, and we went out of Swansea by 5.45 train. At Killay Father and I got out, and Tott went on to Llandovery. Got to the Clerk's house before 8.30. (We met Greening's engine going and coming back, but we had no difficulty in either case.) Got home at 9 pm had supper etc etc.

Saturday 26th – A very wet day. A tremendous gale got up about middle day, the glass was almost down to 'Stormy'. After breakfast read and then went up to Clerk's house and brought down (with new barrow) 5 wraps and a large grocery parcel. After dinner read etc. After tea read.

Sunday 27th – In the morning went up with Mother to the Sunday School, came back and read etc to Maria and Flora. Then went up again to meet Mother. After lunch Father and Mother and I went to Church.

Monday 28th – Father and Mother went to Cyfarthfa Castle. Got up early and took up to the Clerk's house (in new barrow) Father's robe box, a square black box and some wraps. Came back, had some breakfast with them, and then took up (in barrow) the leather portmanteau and two cardboard boxes. They started at 9 am. Then I took the barrow on to the 'Ship' and brought down a box of wine (12 bottles). Soon after I got back I went up to the shop to get some things and got some milk from Mrs Beynon's house. After dinner took the 2 girls out to 'Mary Ann Bevan's gutter' etc (sighting Sheepen Park on the way). After tea we did our scrap books, and I read 'Jack's Courtship'.

Tuesday 29th – (A wet day.) After breakfast went up to the village to get some milk. Came back and read etc with girls. After dinner sighted Sheepen Park etc (very wet). After tea read 'Jack's Courtship' and did different things.
PS – In the afternoon I mended one of Mother's boxes.

Wednesday 30th – (Mother comes home). Went up to Pitton X (before breakfast) and took up a wrap and Mother's old bonnet and muff for William to take into Killay when he went to meet her. I also got some milk. After breakfast took the girls to the sands etc. After dinner took the girls up to George Thomas' house and got 6 eggs, came back, sighted Sheepen Park, gave Maria and Flora a ride in the barrow, made a new perch for the birds etc. Mother came into the kitchen at about 7 pm just before I was going to start to meet her. (She came earlier than we expected).

Thursday 31st – (A wet day.) After breakfast helped Mother to pack my chest. Then went up with the new barrow to the Clerk's house, got the key of the church and cleared away the evergreens. Then brought down Mother's portmanteau, the new coal shovel, wraps and umbrella and a cardboard box. After dinner Mother and I finished packing my chest, and at 5 pm Tom and I took it up (in old wheelbarrow – I pulled). After tea did my scraps etc etc. We rather expected Father but he did not come.

During the summer of 1884 Tottenham was recovering from a serious illness. The Rector describes the journey home from School on that occasion:

Rhosili Rectory,
May 5/84

My dear Charles,
 I knew your Mother would give an account to you from Llandovery from time to time as to Tott. Well, being summoned by yr Mother to help to bring Tott home I went to Llandovery last Wednesday leaving clk's ho at 3.15. Left Killay by last train for Llandovery about 6; got there at 7.40. Yr Mother met me. Thursday the intended day proved too wet & cold so Tott was not allowed to go. I stayed at the Castle. On Friday morning however, wind having veered to SW- off we went. Mr Edwards carried Tott downstairs to George's bus in which (*all day* in a

recumbent position) he went to the station; then off we
went in a first class carriage. Got beautifully to Killay
where we found a roomy close coach and pair waiting. B.
and the porter carried Tott out of train into coach and off
we went, I on box by driver.

Got to Clerk's House in 1¾ hour or less. Lots of people
ready for us. Carried Tott down in easy chair on poles,
raining and blowing all the time. When he got to the
kitchen *I* took him out of the chair & carried him in
triumph upstairs and laid him on his bed. Ever since he has
been home he has continued to improve in every way. Mr
Ellis will give him all needful medical attendance. Will now
daily sit up in chair in bedroom for many hours. I consider
this illness altogether will cost me not less than £70 —
animals all well. 28 sheep in all gone to Hill today. Glad yr
office, in which I take much interest, goes on well.

Yr aff F.

JPL

The Rector always enjoyed writing to his children with any local
news or gossip which he thought might interest them. In July 1893
he wrote to Tottenham:

Rhos. R 23/7/93
Sunday night

My dr Tottenham,

I hasten to communicate some rather rich Peninsula news
or 'Gower Tit-Bits':- On Saturday evening (last night) I
having like all decent people gone to bed at a reasonable
hour Geo Rees of Llangennith appeared in the kitchen with
a doleful tale — yr Mother interviewed him; he kept
beating about the bush, yr Mother keeping on saying Well,
what is it? What is it? At last yr Mother got so frightened
that she said she felt her legs giving way under her! At last
he came to the point. Some people who had been in
Llangennith church (a lot of Swansea workmen) had torn
the surplice all to rags! And poked some of it in the
window of the tower!

It appears that a company which it took 11 horses to
draw came to Llangennith for a picnic — dry dock
engineers co. Well on discovering the damage done Rees
was furious and went to what he calls 'the Committee' and
complained. Upshot was he made the said committee pay
£2 to get a new surplice — which money he brought with
him. No 2. Some of the gang caught sight of Jones of
Barraston's orchard & it being a very good apple season
they conceived the said orchard should be attacked. Jones
did not see it, but fetching his gun aimed it at one fellow &
fired, potting his man. He was shot in the thigh, but not

badly. (Of course Jones had no right to shoot at him under such circumstances). Well they scoured the country for a Doctor; the pellets were extracted & the lad is doing well. But Jones is rather in a scrape, the other side employing a solicitor etc. So by these untoward events the pleasure of their outing was not a little marred and they returned to S'sea in a somewhat lugubrious and crestfallen condition. Rees will on no pretence whatever for the future admit such a crowd or gang into the church or indeed anyone at all without his being present . . . I am in a complete fog as to the day you come home. Tomorrow morn I go to S'sea to meet Loftus from London.

    Yr aff F.

    JPL

Have we perhaps, reading the Rector's letters, penetrated to the reason why it was such a happy and united family at Rhosili Rectory? Here, one might have thought, was the perfect setting for the stock 'Victorian Rectory' situation; a family so isolated from society and a father so much older than his children — the Rector was 43 when Loftus was born, and 54 at the birth of Flora

The Reverend J. P. Lucas.

the youngest — ought not the children to have gone in fear of the stern moralising parent? Yet nothing could be further from the truth. The Rector was a real friend and companion for his children and entered fully and easily into their joys and sorrows. We must remember too that the children adored their mother. Rebecca ran a good home, and 'mother's cooking' became legendary.

There was of course another side to the coin. The children had no social life outside the family circle. Visitors rarely stayed at the Rectory and those that did come provided little companionship for the children. There was Uncle Richard Matthews, Vicar of North Coates in Lincolnshire. He was lively enough but greatly addicted to writing hymn tunes which he would compose on the drawing room piano. Another occasional visitor was Uncle Joseph Matthews, Vicar of Tolmers St Mary in Hertfordshire. He was remembered as of somewhat saintly appearance, tall and thin with deep set eyes and a shining bald head in fascinating contrast to the luxuriance of his beard and side whiskers. His enthusiastic piety was not always expressed in a form likely to appeal to the younger members of the family at Rhosili Rectory. 'Hitherto', he once wrote, 'I have risen each morning at seven. This year I intend, please God, to rise at 5 am, and read a chapter in the Hebrew, a chapter in the Greek Testament, and some thirty pages of some standard work each day.' His enthusiasm for getting up early in the morning led him to write a treatise published in 1855, a thin octavo volume of some 140 pages handsomely printed and bound in gold-tooled imitation leather, entitled *Early Rising. By the Author of* 'What can't be cured must be endured'. Uncle Joseph maintained that rising early in the morning, a time when the air is 'rich in ozone', promotes the health of mind and soul. Between 5 and 6 am was the recommended time. Seven was 'somewhat late' and to rise at 4 am like the late Dr Simeon of Cambridge was, the author conceded, 'very early'. Whether or not it was due to early rising, Joseph Matthews retained his health and vigour into old age and at 74 he could walk as fast and vault a stile as easily as ever. He died in 1911 at the age of 87.

The children had no friends at all of their own age. The reasons were partly geographical and financial. Apart from a few years in the 1880s the Rector had neither horse nor trap and the only means of getting about was on foot, or by hiring a break (an open waggon with bench seats) or on the horse drawn omnibus from Pitton Cross. There were indeed young cousins at Stouthall, about whom I shall say more later, but they lived in a world of great wealth, of horses, grooms, hunting and social occasions, remote from the simple life at Rhosili Rectory: and the Rectory itself was separated in social terms by an unbridgeable gulf from the other families in Rhosili. This was the distinction of class which made it impossible for the Rector's children to make friends in the village. There was of course politeness in the daily round, in church, at choir practice, in the duty calls to people's houses — what Parson Kilvert called 'villaging' — and some friendship and affection arose, but it was strictly circumscribed. It would have been unthinkable for the Rectory children and the village children to meet on equal terms; for Ivor Williams and Willie Gibbs to play cricket with Loftus and Tottenham, for Flora Lucas to go bathing with Lois Beynon. The only exception was the Helme family at Hillend who were 'upper middle class' like the Lucases, but their children were too young to be companions for the children at the Rectory.

This rigid class distinction — absurd snobbishness as it now seems — reflected the age-old divisions of society. It did not seem odd to Victorian eyes that the young girl who worked as maid in that remote Rectory would sit of a winter's evening alone in the kitchen or her tiny back bedroom, while the family sat in the drawing room — except on that rare occasion referred to in Loftus's diary when the Rector 'allowed' Ann to join the family and watch the play. But for the Lucases it was greatly exaggerated by a strong trait in the Rector's character, the overriding importance which he attached to his links with the aristocracy. We have seen how his failure to inherit Stouthall and become a country squire must have rankled. And when a man has no title deeds he must make do with his pedigree. He might not be squire of Stouthall, but at least his mother was a Loftus Tottenham and his Tottenham grandfather had been double first cousin to the Marquis of Ely; and was he not, as he supposed, descended from the family of Sir Charles Lucas of Colchester and Lord Lucas of Shenfield? On odd sheets and scraps of paper my grandfather's impatient handwriting proclaims the titles which flowed so trippingly from his pen: 'Nicholas Loftus, first Viscount Loftus of Loftus Hall married the Honourable Anne Ponsonby daughter of the Viscount Duncannon and sister of the first Earl of Bessborough.' Then there was that 'curious connection between Young and Lucas and the Earl of Milltown' indicating that the Countess of Milltown was his mother's aunt. The Marquises of Ely were particularly reassuring. Was he not himself third cousin to the third Marquis, and his children fourth cousins to the fourth Marquis? 'Dear Father used to say it was very easy to remember', wrote Flora, 'as the cousinship goes the same number always as the number of Marquises.'

There can be no doubt that the Rev J. P. Lucas's sense of his station in life, enhanced by a natural reserve of manner and his determination to ignore the nonconformists which I mentioned earlier, seriously affected his reputation as a parish priest among those of his parishioners who did not know him well, and among Gower people it is to this day, more than eighty years after his death, remembered against him. 'Of course he was County, you had to touch your cap to him.' The story was put about — it was untrue — that for 40 years he never spoke to the postman who delivered the letters to the Rectory. On one occasion, it was said, Mr Bevan of Pitton Cross, a prominent 'Chapel' man, was working in his fields with his son when they saw the Rector approaching on horseback. 'Take no notice of him', said the father, but the son called out 'Good morning Parson'. The Rector riding slowly by ignored them both. This kind of tale was a symptom of the deep divide between church and chapel. One such story we have from the Rector himself, writing to his wife who was away from home:

> My dear R
> Well I reached Killay at 2.13 and started off at 2.30.
> Button was anxiously watching the arrival of the train to
> see if I turned up. I was enabled to do a great favour to a
> young parishioner, thus; at the station I met Olive and
> Margaret Bevan (mantua maker). They came up at once
> and said 'No doubt you did not expect to see us here', then
> Margaret asked if I would be so very kind as to give her a
> seat in my Break for home. Otherwise, she said, she would
> have to wait for hours for one of the omnibuses and then
> she would have to walk from Corner House. Of course I
> assented, only I determined *not to talk* . . . I had a very
> cold drive home. Got to Clerk's house at 5 o'clock. As we
> rattled through the village I thought people eyed my female
> companion! Margaret was of course extremely grateful . . .

This letter was written a few weeks before the Rector's death at the age of 74. This strange reserve, a distaste for the small change of human intercourse, reappears now and again in the family. One is left with a feeling of sadness that the old Rector, such a devoted and affectionate father as we know him to be, felt unable to say anything to the girl sitting with him in the break all through that long cold journey from Killay to Rhosili.

The Cambria loading wood from the wreck of the Helvetia, Rhosili Bay, 1887. Drawing by Tottenham Lucas.

8

1843–1905
Stouthall in the 19th Century —
Lucases, Woods and Crawshays

On the 19th December 1843, in Reynoldston Church, Mary Catherine Lucas (Minnie) the only child of Colonel Lucas and heiress of Stouthall was married to Edward Robert Wood. So came to an end the male succession of Lucases at Stouthall which had continued unbroken, apart from a few years in the 17th century, since Tudor times. The family which for the past four generations had built up its landed wealth by the policy of marrying the eldest son to an heiress now saw all its remaining land in Gower and elsewhere, except Brynfield and a few insignificant acres and cottages, pass into the name of a stranger. Colonel Lucas did make some attempt to preserve the family name by providing in his will that the property should go to his eldest grandchild 'to take the name of Lucas', but this proviso had no legal effect and was ignored. Edward Robert Wood, usually known as Colonel Wood although at the time of his marriage he was no more than a subaltern in the 12th Lancers, was a good looking young man of 23 with dark hair and well-cut features. He had already seen some military service in India where he had taken part in an expedition to map and explore remote areas of the Himalayas in Cashmere. His bride, Minnie, at 20 was in appearance pleasant enough full face but with a heavy profile. She had a rather distant manner and a considerable flair for drawing and painting.

I do not know the origin of the Wood family. It would be romantic to suppose that they were descended from the well-known tribe of Welsh gypsies and harpists of that name, one of whom, John Wood Jones, preceded Griffith as the Llanover family harper. Colonel Wood's parents owned considerable property at Cardiff and near Llandeilo, and the recent history of the Woods was unromantic. The Colonel's father and grandfather, both John Wood, were Cardiff solicitors at a time when the vast expansion of the town was getting under way, an expansion which was to transform Cardiff from little more than a village in the mid

Colonel E. R. Wood of Stouthall,
by Dighton, 1840s.

18th century into the premier city of Wales. John Wood senior had been fortunate to secure one extremely influential client, Lord Mountstewart first Marquis of Bute who had acquired great estates in Glamorgan by marrying into the Herbert family. Wood was an able and ambitious man and with powerful backing held many key positions in Cardiff, Town Clerk, Under Sheriff, Clerk of the Peace, Treasurer of Cardiff Turnpike Trust; and in 1807 he became the principal partner in the Cardiff bank. He was also the object of bitter rivalry and jealousy, and his enemies were quick to exploit what they saw as his mismanagement of charitable and public funds. The second Marquis of Bute lost confidence in Wood and in 1816 appointed one of his principal enemies as agent for the

Mary Catherine Lucas (c.1840)
who married Colonel Wood.

Mountstewart interests. A struggle for power ensued in Cardiff in which both sides used every trick in the book to secure influential positions for their supporters. In 1817 Wood was thrown from his horse while reviewing the Cardiff yeomanry of which he was commander, and died of his injuries. The contest was continued by John Wood junior (1783–1846) who had succeeded to many of his father's appointments, and by his brother Nicholl who was in partnership with him in the Bank.

The battle for the control of Cardiff Corporation came to a head in the Parliamentary election of 1818. The candidate to contest the seat for Cardiff and the associated Boroughs (which included Swansea) on behalf of the Bute faction was the Marquis's brother Lord Patrick James Stewart. The Woods persuaded Lewis Weston Dillwyn of Swansea to stand against him. Dillwyn was well respected and probably would have carried the day, but less than a fortnight before the poll he had to stand down because the Privy Council would not release him from the office of High Sheriff. The Woods in desperation put up their brother Frederick as candidate. The Bute party had thirty 'special constables' sworn in — described by the Woods as 'hired bludgeon men who rushed into the public streets with Lord James's colours in their hats and short poles in their hands, vociferating 'Stewart for Ever!' The Woods are said to have countered by hiring gangs of roughs who stoned several prominent Bute supporters including the candidate himself who was quite badly hurt. In the event Stewart won the day with 45 votes to Wood's 17. From this time on the Bute influence in Cardiff was paramount. Matters now went from bad to worse for the 'Woodlice' as their opponents dubbed them. In 1818 the partnership of John and Nicholl in the Cardiff Bank broke up with a lawsuit between the brothers. The Bank failed in 1823 when John was declared bankrupt and Nicholl fled abroad to avoid his creditors.

John Wood junior's son, Edward Robert, the Colonel, was a man of different stamp from his father and grandfather. He certainly took part in holding public office, as High Sheriff on two occasions, as Justice of the Peace, and as Lieutenant Colonel of the Royal Glamorgan Militia Light Infantry, but he steered clear of local politics. Instead he liked to escape to the solitude of the Gower cliffs where, with one or two workmen from the estate, he excavated several of the Gower bone caves and recovered fossil remains of animals from the pleistocene period. Wood himself had

only an amateurish knowledge of the subject but his friend Hugh
Falconer, who had been with Wood in Cashmere, was well known
as a palaeontologist and botanist and was able to sort and classify
the bones of the strange animals which roamed what is now the
Gower peninsula during the Ice Ages: mammoth and wild ox, cave
bear, hyaena and woolly rhinoceros. Many of Wood's finds are to
be seen in the Royal Institution of South Wales in Swansea.

One guesses that for the Colonel the Gower cliffs were at times
a welcome change from the domesticities of Stouthall where, so it
is said, marital storms were apt to blow up without much warning,
and Minnie Wood was to be seen riding rapidly through the village
on her black mare, with a face of thunder. The Woods had five
daughters, all born during the years 1850 to 1855, Florentia,
Mariana, Charlotte, Catherine and Letitia. In 1861 when the
Colonel was High Sheriff there was a large household at Stouthall
where the resident staff included a Lady's Maid, Governess,
Nurse, Undernurse, Cook, Housemaid, Kitchen Maid, Butler and
Footman. This was in addition to the indoor and outdoor staff who
lived in the villages and came in for the day. At this time the
stables, orchard, kitchen garden, hothouses, flower borders and
shrubberies were managed with an air of military efficiency.
Serious breaches of discipline would be met with instant dismissal,
as on that dreadful day when one of the gardeners was discovered
selling the Colonel's precious nectarines in Swansea market. The
Colonel was, I believe, both loved and feared by his daughters.
One day he was walking in the shrubbery with Florentia. 'Papa,
there is something I have to tell you.' 'Yes, child, what is it?'
'When I went to bed last night I forgot to say my prayers.' 'Well,
say them now.' And the Colonel walked on, leaving Florentia
kneeling among the laurels. The girls are said to have had a happy
childhood, riding their ponies, sketching, arguing, and on Sunday
mornings setting off through the park to Reynoldston Church in a
straggling procession. Catherine always remembered how impossible it was to keep your skirt clean on Easter Sunday when the
villagers, not content with whitewashing the Church, whitewashed
the stiles as well. Catherine tells how the two ancient Gower
customs of the 'Play of St George' and the 'Mari Lwyd' were
observed at Stouthall when she was a child.

> The village youths used to dress up as Mummers at
> Christmas time and go round to the neighbouring houses
> acting. There was one play entitled 'The Play of St George'

in which there were four characters: St George; A Turkish
knight; Father Christmas, a lean figure with a long beard
— very different from the jolly impersonation today; and
lastly the Doctor attired in a black coat and rusty top hat!
St George and the Turkish knight fight with wooden
swords; the Turk falls grievously wounded; but on the
Doctor applying a bottle to his nose arises and walks away.
The drama is concluded.

Then there was the Horse's Head, a most ghastly
apparition! It consisted of a horse's skull bedecked with gay
ribbons; one lad covered in a white sheet forming its body,
and the other leading it with an halter. How they
manipulated its jaws I do not know but it snapped them in
a most terrifying manner; and although we were rather
afraid of it, yet its arrival was always hailed with delight.

Ghost stories were, I think, considered to be topics more suitable
for the servants' hall than for the nursery — at least by the
grown-ups. Florentia, when in later life she was asked about an old
Lucas ghost, replied rather loftily:

There were many ideas abroad among the villagers as to
ladies with powdered hair to be seen in the Upper Park
and I believe someone saw a lady in black of strange
appearance once in the kitchen passage, who disappeared
into the coal cupboard. There was also a wheel of fire in a
tree which an old man (who climbed it to get rooks' eggs)
fell from and was killed. There is a headless horseman seen
sometimes on Cefn Bryn, but I was not aware before that
we were possessed of anything so respectable as a family
bogey.

Colonel Wood as High Sheriff appointed the Rev J. P. Lucas as
his chaplain. This meant that the Rector would have to attend the
opening of the Assizes at Swansea and Cardiff, preach the Assize
Sermon in the Parish Church of each town, and attend the
'Sheriff's Ordinary', a feast provided by the Sheriff for the local
dignitaries. No doubt the fee paid to the chaplain was small but he
would have his expenses paid as well, and it would be a welcome
addition to the Rector's meagre income. The Rector wrote to his
wife from the Cardiff Arms Hotel on 20th July 1861:

My dear Rebecca
I slept Thursday night at Stouthall. Yesterday we got
here by the same train, Sheriff, Judge and Chaplain . . . I
preach tomorrow morn. No doubt the Church will be
crammed. Today I walk over to Llandaff. The judge is Mr
Justice Crompton. He is very agreeable. Colonel Wood & I

dine with him today. Yesterday there was no Sheriff's
Ordinary owing to the death of Col Wood's relative. So
Col Wood, the Under Sheriff, and I dined together at this
hotel where Col Wood and I stay. We ate the following
most greedy Woodish dinner: Turtle soup; salmon;
cucumber; goose; boiled fowls and a ham; peas; kidney
beans; broad beans; potatoes; blancmange; jelly; tarts etc;
cheese; salad; champagne; milk punch; dessert — very fine
grapes, figs, different sorts of fruits etc. I fear your mouths
will water . . . Mrs Wood is not here, nor is she coming.

Next day the Rector reported on the sermon:

The handsome church was completely full — crowded. I
delivered it quite to my own satisfaction. It took 25 minutes
exclusive of the long bidding prayer. Col Wood said I
delivered it if anything rather too slowly but I am glad to
hear this as it was much better than too quick. Col Wood
has pressed me to stay over tomorrow, so I shall not be
home until Tuesday, late no doubt.

Minnie Wood was skilled with brush and pen. It was in 1861
that she completed her *Book of Gower*. This is a series of
watercolour sketches of Gower scenery and buildings, surrounded
by complex and exquisitely finished illuminations in rich enamel
paint. The book shows a strong romantic attachment to Gower,
and its sincerity is in no way diminished by the rather lame verses
which accompany the pictures, composed, according to tradition,
by the Colonel himself.

On the 4th October 1870 took place what must have been the
most elaborate wedding ever seen at Reynoldston, when Florentia
was married to William the eldest son of the ironmaster Robert
Crawshay of Cyfarthfa Castle. This castle, built in 1824 in the
Norman Baronial style is a prominent feature on the skyline
outside Merthyr and opposite the site of the old Cyfarthfa
ironworks. The name Cyfarthfa means 'the place of the barking of
dogs'. Robert Crawshay (1817–79) the 'fourth Iron King' was a
man of great wealth, although by 1870 the trade and prestige of the
ironworks had much declined from the heights achieved under his
father William Crawshay II. The decline was mainly due to the
discovery of the Bessemer steel making process which heralded
the end of the old iron industry. So Robert Crawshay had time to
devote himself to his hobbies. These were, in his earlier years the
Cyfarthfa Workmen's Band, and later photography. In 1860 he
had suffered a stroke which left him stone deaf, so that his family

In Jove most Holy, In Memory most dear.
When Thoughts shall gladden, or Grief excite a tea'
Recalling Pledges at thine Altar made. . . .
Recording where a Kindred dust is laid.

Reynoldston Church 1861, a detail from Mary Catherine Wood's *Book of Gower.*

could only communicate with him by messages usually written on a slate. By the late 1860s he was spending long hours in his studio and dark room at the Castle where his daughter Harriette (known as Trotty) was his unwilling assistant, liable at any time to be summoned to the studio by a blast on her father's whistle. She confided her frustrations to her diary:

> I was taken to be photographed in the afternoon which put me in a bad temper . . . I hate it more than I can tell . . . I was photographed as a fisherwoman with the salmon, and a precious fright I looked . . . Papa came in with the ugliest

dirtiest nastiest old straw bonnet that ever existed, and a
cap . . . for me to be photographed as a fisherwoman . . . I
was photographed with my hair down in wild disorder,
gorgon fashion. Papa says I am a lout not to have kept
steady yesterday being photographed.

The fourth Iron King's wife Mrs Rose Crawshay was a woman of
intellectual tastes. Inspired perhaps by that other Ironmaster's
wife Lady Charlotte Guest who translated the Mabinogion she
sought the company of poets and men of letters. The works of
Byron, Shelley and Keats had a particular fascination for her. Men
of the greatest eminence came to stay at the Castle, were taken for
rows on the lake, and posed for Robert Crawshay's camera — the
visitors included Emerson, Darwin, Herbert Spencer, Robert
Owen, Dean Stanley and Robert Browning. Mrs Crawshay was a
practical philanthropist who did much to help the poor and needy
among her husband's workpeople. She had two enthusiams which
struck her contemporaries as eccentric and indeed shocking;
euthanasia and cremation. She had the preposterous notion that
on her death her body might conveniently be disposed of in one of
the ironworks's furnaces.

The Crawshays had five children; William, Harriette (Trotty),
Henrietta (Pops), Robert and Richard (Tids). The marriage of
William and Florentia seems to have met with approval in both
families. Negotiations for the all important financial settlements
were concluded in good time. By one of the Settlements the whole
of the Stouthall estate in Gower was settled on Florentia for life,
subject to a life interest for her mother, and in the event, as
Florentia and William had no children, the estate went to
Florentia absolutely. There were three trustees of this settlement,
two of them being solicitors and the third the Rev J. P. Lucas of
Rhosili. Florentia, who was 21 at the date of the marriage was a
plainish rather serious-minded girl. She had been taught the
necessary social skills, was a good rider, a keen card player, but
somewhat lacking in grace. Her fiancé was an athletic young man,
a good games player and a crack shot.

The wedding took place on the 4th October 1870. We have two
descriptions of it, one from Mr Roland Bevan of Horton who
walked over to Reynoldston to watch the fun, and the other from
the *Cambrian* newspaper. The article in the *Cambrian* is unsigned,
but the style seems unmistakable, and I believe that students of
Gower literature will recognise the pen of that delightful old

'Genius of Gowerland' C. D. Morgan, author of *Wanderings in Gower* first published in the 1860s. It is not surprising that Morgan who lived in Parkmill should have been asked to report the wedding as he was at this time a contributor to the *Cambrian* and was well known to Mr Williams its proprietor.

Bevan was first on the scene. He tells us that in an early morning rehearsal the Reynoldston bellringers succeeded in cracking one of the two church bells in their enthusiasm to make the most of what must have been at best a very limited peal. Bevan's account is, as one would expect, a good deal more down to earth than the *Cambrian*. Where the paper tells us that 'the booming of artillery echoed from hill to hill' Bevan remarks drily that 'someone found an old cannon and set it off'. The first big moment of the day occurred when the church was already filled with an unwonted collection of fashionables. This was the arrival of the bridegroom 'in a chariot drawn by six white horses with postillions and outriders'. Bevan does not tell us how many miles of Gower roads had been negotiated by this splendid equipage. The bride arrived with her father from Stouthall in the family coach drawn by two new greys. At this point I hand over — if I am right about him — to C. D. Morgan, for what must surely be an outstanding example of mid 19th century provincial journalism:

> The interesting and pleasing ceremony was performed in the presence of a fashionable assemblage in Reynoldston Church, by the Rev Wm Lucas Collins MA Vicar of Kilsby . . . Uncle-in-law of the bride, assisted by the Rev John Ponsonby Lucas, Rector of the Parish (sic) and the Rev John Hughes, Curate. The church was tastefully decorated with evergreens formed into various devices. The young and beautiful bride was received in the church by the bridegroom and his 'best man' (Mr Arthur Crawshay, Dan-y-Park). She was attired in white satin, having an elegant train flounced with Brussells lace, with a veil of the same rich material. The dress was trimmed with orange blossoms. She wore a magnificent diamond necklace and earrings, the gift of Mr Crawshay of Cyfarthfa Castle; one bracelet of emeralds and diamonds presented by Colonel Wood's Carmarthenshire tenantry; and the other of diamonds and carbuncles, presented by his Gower tenantry. She was attended by her bridesmaids, four of whom were her sisters, and the other two were the sisters of the bridegroom. They were attired in pink and white. Each wore a handsomely designed locket, bearing the monogram of the bride and bridegroom.

After the marriage service had been gone through, and
Mr William Thompson Crawshay and Miss Florentia Maria
Wood had been pronounced 'Man and Wife' and the
necessary documents signed, the bridal party left the
Church. As they proceeded along the avenue from the
porch to the road, both sides of which were lined by the
school children (the little boys wearing blue navy shirts,
white trousers and white straw hats, the little girls being
clad in scarlet cloaks), the little fellows cheered the happy
couple with right good will, as loud and vigorously as their
lungs would permit, while the little girls, in the
characteristic simplicity of rustic happiness, strewed the
path with flowers — the whole presenting a scene as
beautiful as it was touching.

The cheering of *ces petits enfants* was taken up by a
crowd of eager spectators, anxious to behold the heir of
Cyfarthfa Castle, who had that day come to take to her
future home one of the most amiable and accomplished
daughters of Gowerland — a favourite flower in the
parterre of Stouthall which, when transplanted to another
soil, will bloom, we doubt not, with fresh radiance.

After the marriage ceremony, a select company
assembled at Stouthall to do honour to Mr W. Thompson
Crawshay and Mrs Crawshay, where a magnificent *dejeuner*
was laid.

After the health of the bride and bridegroom had been
proposed and responded to, and other complimentary
toasts given, the pleasing ceremony was brought to a close
at one o'clock by the happy pair leaving, in a carriage
drawn by four greys, with mounted postillions, for Swansea
en route for their marriage tour. Their departure took
place amidst the throwing of a multitude of slippers and
rice, kindly greetings, and hopes that perpetual harmony
may attend their path.

The day was as beautifully bright as could have only
been expected at midsummer; and as the unobscured sun
shone upon the autumnal foliage which threw its broad
shades upon the grassy bed beneath, it reflected a
combination of tints whose harmony gave a floral lustre to
all around. The songsters of the grove and forest threw out
their liveliest notes, as though they were conscious of the
great event of the day, and all nature seemed united in
doing honour to the occasion. The husbandman and
peasant left their daily avocations, laid aside their
implements of industry, and went forth to assist in the
general rejoicing. Such was the happy condition of
Reynoldston and its neighbourhood upon the occurrence of
this auspicious event. The smiling village was arched and
festooned with flowers and evergreens bearing appropriate

mottoes and devices. The gate entrances to the family
mansion were also arched with nature's decorations. 'The
lads and lasses wore their favours white and the village
bells did ring'. The booming of artillery echoed from hill to
hill, and the merry makings were not brought to an end
until the shades of evening had settled upon the landscape.
A grand ball was given in the evening at Fairy Hill in
honour of the event, and the *esprit de dance* was kept up to
a late hour.

The paper goes on to describe the celebrations at Glais in the
Swansea valley where 'the good people are, have long been, and
continue to be warm *attachés* of the Lucases of Stouthall.' Guns
were fired in a *feu de joie* on the Garth field and free beer was
provided, in spite of which 'everything passed off without any
unpleasantness'. At Merthyr there were four separate celebrations, one for the 'principal tradesmen'; one for 'gentlemen of the
neighbourhood'; one for senior employees of the ironworks; and
one for the schoolchildren. For the latter there was 'an ample
supply of tea and cake, after which a Panorama of the War was
exhibited.' In Merthyr market place 'the celebrated Cyfarthfa
Band played a number of choice *morceaux*'.

Roland Bevan tells us that as the guests for the party at Fairyhill
drove through Reynoldston Lower Green 'fireworks were let off
by the villagers. These fireworks were very primitive being balls of
shoemakers' hemp soaked in turpentine which were thrown from
hand to hand across the road. They were made by Mr Harris who
kept the Post Office. Several days after the wedding all the village
children were entertained to tea at Stouthall'.

The *Cambrian* contained a long list of wedding presents. The
diamond necklace from Robert Crawshay was 'splendid', the
bridegroom gave the bride 'a magnificent dressing case', and
another 'magnificent' present was a gold casket from the Bensons
at Fairyhill. Mrs Crawshay's gifts seem to tail off: 'a set of pearls, a
very handsome china toilet, a bread trencher and knife, and
illuminated blotting book'. The Crawshay governess gave grape
scissors and the Wood governess what is laconically described as 'a
book'. Whatever my grandparents from Rhosili Rectory may have
given to mark the occasion was not deemed worthy of mention by
the *Cambrian*.

For a few years after the wedding there were happy family
gatherings at Stouthall. Trotty in particular found them a relief
from the horrors of her father's studio. In her diary for May 1871

she writes:

> May 22 . . . For a wonder I was let go to Stouthall with
> Tids, William and Flora (Florentia) for 3 days. I enjoyed it
> very well but was not able to get about much. We took our
> lunch to Mewslade one day but I was so knocked up by the
> time we got down to the rocks that I could not eat any
> lunch and was obliged to lie on the rocks for 3 hours before
> I felt better, but then I enjoyed it very much. The spray
> from the waves dashing against the rocks was lovely. Once
> it dashed all over William, Tids and Flora who thought
> they were standing at a safe distance. Then William and
> Tids amused us by seeing who could get out on a bit of
> rock which the waves came over, and stay longest without
> getting wet altogether . . . Flora was such a dear to me
> while I did not feel well.

Trotty did eventually escape from the confines of Cyfarthfa
Castle, married happily, and lived to be 92. Her father died in
1879. He is buried in Vaynor churchyard near Merthyr, a tiny
crowded churchyard on a steep hillside. Perhaps mindful of his
wife's notion of being cremated in the Cyfarthfa furnace, he took
precautions to ensure that his own remains should rest undisturbed. His grave is covered with a single slab of granite twelve
feet long by eight feet wide, and fifteen inches thick. It is inscribed
simply with his name, age and date of death, and the words *God
Forgive Me*. People have wondered which particular sins he had in
mind.

Colonel Wood died after a short illness in 1876 at the early age
of 57. Minnie and her four unmarried daughters soon afterwards
left Stouthall never to return. Later Mariana married the
Honourable Charles Hore-Ruthven, Catherine married James
Laidlaw and Letitia married Francis Villiers Bruce. The story goes
that Minnie had planned for Catherine to marry a middle-aged
parson, but Catherine had other ideas and eloped with her riding
master James Laidlaw. The disappointed suitor set off in pursuit,
armed in the best traditions of Victorian melodrama with a horse
whip, but the couple eluded him and were happily married.

During the early years of their marriage William and Florentia
lived at Vaynor House near Merthyr. They moved into Cyfarthfa
Castle in 1880 where, sad to say, the 'favourite flower in the
parterre of Stouthall' never bloomed with that fresh radiance so
confidently predicted by the *Caml rian*. Florentia did not like the
Castle. William converted the Ironworks at great expense to steel

making, but his heart was not in the business. In 1889 they left the Castle for good and made their home at another Crawshay mansion, Caversham Park near Reading. In 1896 Florentia became a Catholic. The *Cambrian* was shocked and reported the event in tones appropriate to the discovery of scandal in high places:

> Various rumours have prevailed respecting the secession from the Protestant Church of a lady well known in Glamorgan society, but the facts of the case have not been thoroughly stated. It may now be accepted as authentic that Mrs William Crawshay, the wife of the well known Ironmaster of Cyfarthfa, has openly embraced the Roman Catholic Faith . . . Mrs Crawshay remained at Cyfarthfa Castle for some time after the death of Mr Robert Crawshay and the retirement of Mrs Rose Mary Crawshay, but was never thoroughly identified with the social life of the Iron Metropolis, and since the retirement of the family to Caversham Park there has been almost a complete sunderance.

William died in 1918 — in his last illness a convert to the Catholic faith — and Florentia survived him for little more than a year. She was remembered at Caversham for her generosity to the local Catholic Church and for her children's Christmas parties for the

Stouthall in 1935, much as it stands today.

pupils of the Catholic school. By her will she left the Stouthall estate to her nephew Charles Hore-Ruthven and his children. It was decided that the property should be sold, and all that remained of the old Stouthall estate of the Lucases was put under the hammer in July 1920. It included many farms, cottages and other properties, 1040 acres in all divided into 236 lots. Many of the farms and cottages were bought by their tenants.

Between Colonel Wood's death in 1876 and 1920 Stouthall was let to a variety of tenants, among them the Vulliamy family who often rented the house for their summer holidays. Mr C. E. Vulliamy the author, who was 10 years old in 1896 has recorded his memories of Stouthall:

> Between the years 1889 and 1904 my father used occasionally to rent this delightful mansion, and it was here, in the pleasant leisure of summer days, that I spent the happiest hours of my life . . . Probably when I lived there I did not realise the immense debt, the accident of good fortune which I owed to Stouthall.
>
> In the splendid oval room there was a library. No doubt there were much better libraries in other country mansions, but this was my first experience of a large private collection of books; indeed it was my first experience of literature. Below the shelves were glass cases full of bones and other fossils from the Gower caves. On one side of the library there were doors artfully disguised as book-shelves, through which you could escape to the drawing-room when you heard visitors approaching the front door.
>
> The Stouthall books covered a wide range: poetry, art, science, drama, history, archaeology, sport, fiction, and even the elegant philosophy of *Humboldt's Cosmos*. I now realise that there were many strange absences, and the taste of the collectors, though invariably sound, was always discreet and orthodox: it was not the taste of litterateurs or of unhampered bachelors: one had to think of wives or daughters and the awful risks of contamination. Thus, although Thomas Moore was on the shelves, Byron was represented only by his bust: Dickens was there in full force, but you would have looked in vain for George Eliot or Charlotte Bronte, though you would have discovered the complete works of Lever and of Bulwer Lytton. Still, I learnt a good deal about the facts of life (greatly to my astonishment and advantage) from the first edition of the *Encyclopaedia Britannica*.
>
> My parents never sat or entertained their guests in the drawing-room, but always in the library. So I appropriated the drawing-room for my own use. Neither its furniture nor

its pictures were in any way remarkable. There were here two scrap books, so large that I could hardly lift them, full of coloured prints and etchings dating from the late 18th century to the period of the earliest railways; a source of delight, amusement and instruction.

In the lofty hall hung portraits of the Lucas family, none of them by first rate painters. Colonel Wood himself was magnificently represented in the dining room, looking very fine with his curling dark hair and his moustaches and the noble uniform of a cavalry officer. Here also was an elderly military gentleman known as 'General Lucas' and a lamentably accurate full-size copy of Landseer's *Monarch of the Glen*. You passed from the dining room across a small vestibule, to the billiard room (admirably equipped for the game) and thence to the smoking-room or the gun-room with its garden door. The kitchen block including the original servants' rooms (rotting in a sinister green gloom), extended from the main block at a lower level concealed, without regard for light or convenience, by a thicket of shrubs.

A gallery, to which you ascend by a graceful curving stairway, runs round three sides of the hall, and from this gallery you entered the principal bedrooms and their dressing rooms. On the floor above were the smaller bedrooms and the nursery with its collection of 18th and early 19th century toys — dusty dolls, exquisitely carved models of Swiss chalets, lustrous globes and little mandarin figures which impressed me with a strange appearance of melancholy and reproach, dangling dimly in the dark recesses of their cupboard.

Stouthall was a fine house: yet the conditions under which we lived there would strike most of the young people of today, and even some of their elders, as almost repulsively primitive. There was no laid-on supply of drinking water, no main drainage, only one water closet, no means of obtaining light except from paraffin lamps or candles, no hot water in your room unless it was brought there in a tin can, no such thing as a bath-room, no means of heating any part of the house except by open fires in grates. The drinking water had to be fetched every morning in two casks from the spring in Reynoldston, and these casks were usually carried by a donkey. All haulage was by horses, and the only car which I ever saw at Stouthall was a steam driven car which conveyed a doctor from Swansea on the occasion of my mother's illness: it was a quiet elegant vehicle, only hissing softly when the engine took up the load, and before the doctor left we had to bring down all the water jugs from the bedrooms to fill his tank.

I have put the house and the library first, but I think the

most vivid and living of all my Stouthall memories are
those of the grounds and the gardens which were then of
extraordinary beauty — a beauty altogether informal, the
result of a happy balance between the care of man and the
exuberance of nature. Here, invaded by trees and
undergrowth, were the Gothic stone fantasies (known as
'the caves') erected by an early romantic Lucas; here was
the cool grotto with its green and yellow crystals; the cork
tree; the masses of many coloured rhododendrons; the
sundial, the stone urn and the pampas grass. There was a
vast walled garden for fruit and vegetables, and a hothouse
— the pride of Mr Ace, the Wood's gardener — where
clustered grapes, the red or the muscatelle, were to be had
for the asking. Mr Ace was a tall majestic figure, bearded,
bright-eyed, like the men so often painted and etched by
Rembrandt; having more natural nobility, I think, than any
other man I have met in the whole course of my life.

The Woods are commemorated in the west window of Reynoldston Church, given by Florentia in 1905 in memory of her parents. It
was designed by Nathaniel Westlake, a well known art historian and
designer of church windows. It is, in an enigmatic way, a memorial
to Florentia herself, as the central figure is her birthday saint, St
Barnabas. There is a scene from the life of a Carmelite nun, St
Maria of Florence, a play not on her mother's names but her own.
Her father's name, Edward, is suggested by St Edward the
Confessor. The window was dedicated on St Barnabas' day,
Whitsunday, 1905, and Florentia was invited to attend. She
declined, on the grounds of her husband's ill health. Was there a
deeper reason why she did not want to come to Reynoldston, which
would have meant a visit to Stouthall? Why, for that matter, did
none of the girls or their mother ever come back? The house and
grounds were maintained in perfect order for many years after
Colonel Wood's death. The family portraits still hung on the walls,
the family books filled the shelves in the charming library, the
children's toys gathered dust in the nursery cupboard. In the
hothouses the grapes were as luscious as ever. Yet nobody came;
except a few strangers for the summer holidays. The house may
have been too old fashioned for them. Or were there, perhaps,
more bogeys at Stouthall than Florentia cared to admit?

9

1882–96
The Clipper Ship Middlesex
and the Wreck of the Danmark

In September 1882 Loftus, aged 15, left Llandovery School and donned the blue jacket with anchor buttons and gold braided collar of a cadet on the school ship Conway. He carried with him a letter from Dr Edwards:

> Master Loftus Tottenham Lucas has been a pupil in the school for the last six years. I can speak in the very highest terms of his character. He is a thoroughly reliable and trustworthy boy; and he is in every sense of the word a gentleman. I have no hesitation in strongly recommending him for any position where intelligence and reliability are required.

Loftus had always felt the call of the sea strongly. I do not know whether his parents tried to dissuade him from his chosen career, though they probably had misgivings over the long separations and the dangers and uncertainties of a life at sea. The Gower coast in those days was a graveyard of ships and sailors. Rebecca would hardly have forgotten that stormy night in 1879 when the sailing ship Mary Stenhouse went aground in Rhosili bay, and the bodies of the Captain's wife and ten of the crew were washed up on the beach below the Rectory. Loftus, of course, looked forward to his new life with boyish enthusiasm.

The Conway training scheme had been founded in 1858 by the Mercantile Marine Association with the object of training boys to become officers in the Merchant Service. The Admiralty had provided two old frigates, first the Conway and later the Winchester to be moored as school ships in the Mersey, but the scheme proved so successful that a larger ship was needed. In 1875 the Navy handed over an old battleship the Nile which had been launched in 1839. She was a 91-gun ship-of-the-line and had seen active service in the Baltic during the Crimean war. Now, fully rigged but with her guns removed, and re-named Conway, she was moored at Rockferry in the Mersey. When Loftus joined her she was the home of some 160 cadets aged from 13 to 18. The course of study was usually for two years, during which the boys spent about half their working day on ordinary school subjects, history, geography, English, French and mathematics. The rest of their time was spent on elementary seamanship and engineering, navigation and meteorology.

A few boys joined the Navy on completing the Conway course, but most the Merchant Service. For the latter a Conway certificate counted as a year at sea, and the successful cadet could take his first Board of Trade examination for second mate after three years apprenticeship at sea instead of the usual four. Life on the Conway was tough; the boys were divided into two watches, slept in hammocks and were under strict naval discipline. In some respects the training was old fashioned. The naval rigging on which the boys were taught had been obsolete in the Merchant Service for at least ten years when Loftus joined. But the Conway had a high reputation for smartness and discipline, for a thorough grounding in navigation, and for an ability to handle small boats.

During the 1880s British Merchant Shipping was fairly equally divided between sail and steam. In 1885 of all ships entering the port of Swansea 2344 were steamers and 2634 under sail. The total tonnage of British ships was double that of the rest of the world, and the world's busiest port was Liverpool. The scene on the Mersey has been described by another old Conway boy, some ten years younger than Loftus, the poet John Masefield, who writes of his time on the Conway in the 1890s:

> The flower of all England's shipping belonged to Liverpool; the river and docks were always busy with the best ships of the time. The Cunard moorings were just down stream of us; the White Star and Inman moorings beyond them . . . The steamers of many famous lines were weekly visitors to the river, we knew them all, their funnels, their house flags and their tenders; even the foreign steamers and what they brought were known to us.
>
> But in those days the bulk of the world's freight was carried in sailing ships, which had then reached their last, strange, beautiful perfection. At all times we could see in the river or in the docks the queens of that last construction, the superb four masted ships and barques, of

from two to three thousand tons . . . They are now gone,
but then they were many; and many of them were strange
with new device of build or rig, of intense interest to us
whose talk and thought was of ships.

Often, perhaps every week, sometimes for weeks
together every day, one such queen would come with her
tugs into the Sloyne and anchor near us, all trim from her
last month's work, her sails in harbour stows, her blocks
gleaming, her mainyards still aback, just as they had braced
them on taking the tow line, and her house flag at her main
truck. Then at the next flood her crowd would man the
capstan, her anchor would come in to 'Rolling Home' or
'Goodbye, Fare you well', and she would pass to dock . . .
For beauty interest and variety no scene on earth could
compare with the river in which we lived. We were in the
sea world and of it, initiated into the mystery and free of
the guild, and there at its busiest heart. Of all the many
joys that youth and ship offered, that gift of beauty was the
greatest.

Loftus shared John Masefield's vision of the sea and of the
beauty and romance of the sailing ship, and it is not surprising that
he chose to serve his apprenticeship in sail, in one of the famous
clipper ships.

The Middlesex was the last and the largest of a fine fleet of
sailing ships owned by George Marshall & Sons. She was launched
on the Clyde, at the Glasgow shipyard of Barclay Curle & Co.in
November 1884, a few weeks before Loftus completed his service
on the Conway. On 1st January 1885 he was apprenticed for three
years to Marshalls, and in February he joined the Middlesex for
her maiden voyage to Australia. She was built with an iron hull,
three masted, a considerably larger ship than the tea clippers, of
which the Cutty Sark is the one best known to modern readers.
The Middlesex was 255 feet long, her mainmast from truck to deck
was 162 feet, and her yards 88 feet wide. By comparison the Cutty
Sark was 212 feet long with a 145 foot mainmast.

Middlesex carried two apprentices, Loftus and a lad named
Clarkson; 'Quite a gentleman', Loftus reported to his parents, 'I
think we shall get on well together'. On this maiden voyage to
Sydney, the Middlesex carried a mixed cargo. Loftus helped to
load 'drain pipes, flooring boards, pig iron, and hundreds of casks
of I don't know what'. In fact many of the casks contained
gunpowder, something which Loftus refrained from mentioning.
He also helped to stow the Captain's provisions, 'Every imagin-

able kind of potted meat, fish, pickles, biscuits, things to make puddings of, an immense quantity of jams and preserved fruits, wines etc etc (really quite wonderful) and I believe they are all supplied by the owners!'

After waiting for several days at the 'Tail o'the Bank' off Greenock for a wind the Middlesex finally left the Clyde on 14th February 1885, and after a further fifty miles tow the tug cast off and the Middlesex set sail for Sydney. The pilot was put ashore at the Tuskar rock off south east Ireland taking with him the crew's final letters home. Thereafter, apart from being 'spoken' by a brigantine off the coast of Portugal, who reported her safe and well, the Middlesex for the rest of her voyage was entirely cut off from the world.

In his sea chest, already well stocked with delicacies supplied by his mother, Loftus carried several last minute presents from the family. These included from his mother a sheet of pens, a bottle of ink, cotton wool and buttons; from Flora a tiny china cottage; and from Tottenham some carefully drawn plans on paper backed with linen, of Rhosili, Middleton and Pitton, with the houses marked and the name of the occupant of each house, bound up in brown

The Middlesex.

paper and measuring no more than five inches square. This little book is entitled 'Plans of a few little villages in west Gower. To my dear brother to remind him on his voyages of our old home, with love from his affectionate brother Tottenham. January 1885.' In fact Loftus needed no reminding. He suffered little from sea-sickness, but he was home-sick, a malady from which he suffered throughout his sea career. His letters home are full of concern for events at the Rectory, and particularly for Rap his terrier puppy. 'I hope dear old Rap gets on all right. Please kiss him from me . . . will you please, dear Father, give Rap fresh straw in his kennel *every other Monday*. I changed it yesterday week, so next Monday will be the day . . . to night you will have to get the wood down from the loft for the first time . . . Did you notice what I did to the rockwork? I put a layer of stones all along the top. It is a great protection to the garden . . .'

The Middlesex was under the command of Captain George Janes, a very experienced master for whom Loftus had great respect. The crew on this voyage were a rough crowd, who had signed on for the round trip, but most of whom intended to desert as soon as the ship reached Australia where they reckoned they could earn better wages. Captain Janes intended to show them from the start that he would stand no nonsense. Much of the ship's work was traditionally accompanied by sea shanties. The Captain ordered the men not to introduce indecent versions of these songs, but when the anchor was being heaved up to the tune of 'Sally Brown' the shanty man sang just such a line. No sooner were the words out of his mouth than Captain Janes strode up and felled him to the deck with a single blow. The man picked himself up and silently resumed his place at the capstan bars, while another man took up a more respectable solo.

The sea routes to the Far East had been greatly shortened by the opening of the Suez canal in 1869, but the cost of the canal dues and the long towage were considered excessive for most sailing ships, which continued to use the traditional route round the Cape of Good Hope. Once round the Cape on the outward voyage the ships would pick up the westerly winds of the southern ocean, the 'roaring forties', for running their easting down. On this first voyage Captain Janes took the Middlesex well south of the Cape in his search for a good wind, but conditions were unusual, with light airs and thick weather; until on 25th April in latitude 50 degrees far to the south of Cape Leeuin in western Australia, the weather changed with a vengeance. One of the jobs of the apprentices was to handle some of the highest sails on the ship. Loftus and Clarkson would have been working aloft in the conditions which the Captain described:

> On April 25th . . . the ship fell in with a heavy gale from the westward. There was a high sea with the storm and the vessel laboured heavily and shipped large bodies of water . . . On the 26th without any warning, the wind shifted suddenly from west to south south west and blew with hurricane force. The ship was kept dead before the wind. An attempt was made to take in the main topgallant sails and upper fore and main topsails, but before this could be done they were blown to ribbons. At 2 am the ship was brought to the wind. Heavy seas broke on board with great violence and flooded the decks fore and aft. The lee side was filled level with the rails, and sail room and deck houses were flooded. At 2.30 am the screw box on the steering gear gave way, but the tiller was secured with tackle. The gale blew with hurricane violence until 4 am by which time it settled into a heavy south west gale accompanied by hail and snow squalls. While hauling the main yards, in bringing the ship to the wind, the lower main topgallant yard was sprung. Soon after, the port clew of the mainsail and outer jib were blown adrift and damaged considerably. At noon there was a strong gale blowing but towards sundown the weather moderated.

Although Captain Janes does not mention it in this account which he gave to a Sydney newspaper, the loss of the sails was not due to any misjudgment on the part of the Captain, but to the refusal by some of the crew to obey orders and go aloft at the critical moment. The Middlesex entered Sydney harbour at 8 am on May 7th after a passage of 78 days from pilot to pilot, accounted a very fast time. She berthed on the following day, after first unloading the barrels of gunpowder at a secluded spot. That night the crew broached a barrel of rum and engaged in a riotous blind. Pandemonium reigned on board and in the small hours of the morning Captain Janes sent Loftus to fetch the water police. The officers were not sorry when within a few days the whole crew had vanished along the Sydney water front and were seen no more.

In his first letter home sent with the pilot at the Tuskar rock, Loftus had reported 'I still think the Captain and officers very nice, but best of all the Captain of his own accord has turned those three boys into the Forecastle, and Clarkson and I have this cabin all to ourselves.' Writing from Sydney, Loftus confirms his good opinion of the Captain, but 'the mate I am sorry to say is far from what I first took him to be.' Letters from home were waiting at Sydney when the Middlesex docked, having no doubt come by the Suez canal. Loftus reported to his parents:

> I never felt better in my life than I do at the present moment . . . So far I like the sea *quite* as much as I thought I should. Of course I found the work very hard at first, but soon got accustomed to it. At sea we *never* have more than 3½ hours sleep at a time. Our rations while at sea are: Weekly — 1 lb sugar (each), ½ lb butter, 1 lb marmalade, and a little vinegar. Daily — 1 lb salt meat or ¾ lb salt pork (including bone), some potatoes and soup, also ¾ lb bread every Tuesday and Friday (ie what the cook calls bread) instead of potatoes; and ½ lb tinned bully beef and the same amount of duff on Sundays, which is merely dough boiled with a few raisins instead of baked; and as much hard tack (biscuit) in reason as we want. Also one small tin condensed milk between two per week. The quality of the pannikin of tea in the evening and coffee in the morning beggars description! I can manage to drink the tea but I cannot drink the coffee at all. In port however it is much worse as we get nothing besides 1½ lbs fresh mutton (which is 2d per lb here) except of course the potatoes and soup for dinner; so that if we want butter or bread, or anything of that sort, we have to buy it ourselves. For the first few weeks I could not eat any of the meat, it is so *very* salt, but I could eat a little for some time before we arrived. But we all thrive!

The Middlesex remained berthed at Sydney for a month. The Rector had hoped that Loftus would be able to call on his distant relative Lord Loftus then Governor General of Australia. Loftus did call at Government House and made an appointment, but he was unable to keep it as the ship received unexpected orders to proceed in ballast to Chittagong to load a cargo of jute. She sailed on June 8th, her chosen route being up the east coast of Australia and through the Torres straits between Australia and New Guinea. Navigation through the maze of islands and reefs in the straits was tricky and it was not considered safe to be under way at night. But when stopped there was a considerable risk of being boarded by pirates. Captain Janes's plan for dealing with pirates was to set fire to them. Red hot ashes were kept ready in the donkey house and tins of paraffin were distributed along the deck under the bulwarks; but the Middlesex got through the straits unmolested. There were two deaths on this voyage. The saloon steward 'who had broached a rum cask three times and been let off an equal number of times broached it for the fourth time'. While being taken before the Captain he made a dash for the side and leapt overboard. A buoy was thrown to him and the gig lowered but no trace of him was found in the shark-infested waters.

> On the Wednesday week before we arrived (wrote Loftus)
> Mr Webster the passenger, a nice fellow about my own
> age, complained of violent pains in the stomach. He turned
> in early that night, and died on the following Friday night
> from a 'stoppage in the bowels' having been laid up only 48
> hours. The Captain asked Clarkson and me to stay with
> him in turns during our watch on deck, and it was during
> my watch that he died poor fellow. You can imagine what
> a very sad affair it was, the poor Captain was *much
> distressed*. He was buried on Saturday morning, the service
> being read by the mate.

The Middlesex made Chittagong, in the bay of Bengal near the borders of India and Burma, after a passage of 54 days. She remained moored there in the river from the 7th August to the 26th October. Conditions on the river, in the steamy monsoon heat, must have been almost intolerable for those living within the ship's iron hull. Loftus in his long letters home says little about the conditions except to remark 'It is terribly hot here and the mosquitos are a dreadful pest. I am bitten all over.'

Captain Janes had brought 20 sheep from Australia as a speculation. Loftus and Clarkson had each bought rosella birds in Sydney; and by the time she left Chittagong the ship's menagerie included four monkeys, two parrots, one cockatoo, eight rock minas, two rosellas and a mongoose. Letters from home arrived on the British India Company's mail steamers. The Rector wrote with tit bits of local news and Rebecca sent a diary of each day's events at home, which she had kept specially to send to her son. During September and October the Middlesex loaded over 13 000 bales of jute which had been brought 800 or 900 miles down river in brigs, each of which carried 500–1000 bales. During October a sailing ship moored just ahead of the Middlesex. She was the Mary Stenhouse of Liverpool which had run aground in Rhosili Bay in 1879. During their time at Chittagong the only relief from the drudgery and boredom for the two apprentices was an occasional Sunday service held by the British chaplain on one or other of the many British ships moored there, followed by tea at the Chaplain's house. Once the boys took a short trip to see a captured wild elephant.

On October 26th the Middlesex sailed for Dundee, rounding the Cape of Good Hope and later the north of Scotland to avoid easterly winds in the English channel. She arrived in Dundee early in March. Loftus made two more voyages in the Middlesex. In each case she loaded coal at Cardiff in May and set sail for Singapore, a voyage of over 90 days. From Singapore she went on to Chittagong for jute, arriving there in November, a much cooler and pleasanter time of the year. At the end of November she left Chittagong for Dundee. In 1886/7 this passage took only 121 days 'one of the smartest of the season'. It was at Chittagong in 1886 that Loftus heard that his father had bought a pony trap, news which he found so exciting that he lay awake at night thinking about it. He loved animals, particularly dogs and horses. In his letters home, as well as greetings to various village people he almost always sent 'my compliments to the animals'.

On Loftus's third and last voyage in the Middlesex, three weeks before reaching Singapore, he fell from aloft and broke his left thigh. There was no doctor aboard, and he was indeed lucky that Captain Janes had a strong interest in things medical and knew a good deal about first aid. He set the thigh so successfully that when the Middlesex reached Singapore the Doctor said he was entirely satisfied with the Captain's treatment. Loftus made a perfect recovery, apart from a slight limp due to a half inch shortening of the leg, and his strong powers as a walker remained unimpaired. He left the Middlesex at Dundee in March 1888 at the end of his apprenticeship. Clarkson, not being a Conway boy, had to serve for a further year; and on the Middlesex's fourth voyage out to the Far East he fell to his death from the weather fore yard-arm.

Captain Janes retired from the sea a few years later. Beneath a brusque manner he was a kindly man, and Clarkson's death troubled him. His letter to Loftus about Clarkson's family was probably typical of him.

> . . . I have had to see Clarkson's brother and sister. They are a little touched, especially the sister; but as poor Clarkson leaves £2500 to be divided between them they will, I expect, soon recover. I expressed my feelings pretty freely about his ever being allowed to follow the sea at all; however he is away from them and will be no more trouble.

Soon afterwards Marshalls sold the Middlesex to new owners, who kept her old name. On September 30th 1895 she sailed from Samarang in East Java bound for New York with a cargo of palm sugar. She was sighted at St Michael's in the Azores on January 21st 1896, but was never seen again, and was posted at Lloyds as a missing vessel in May of that year.

After leaving the Middlesex, Loftus passed his first Board of Trade examination and in January 1889 he was appointed third officer to the steamship Missouri on her maiden voyage from West Hartlepool to Baltimore. Missouri was one of a fleet of steamers owned by the Atlantic Transport line. They were mainly cargo vessels, although some took passengers also, and were employed on the north Atlantic service from London to Baltimore, Philadelphia and New York. The ships were British built with British crews, but American owned and financed. Loftus served with this Company for 17 years. Missouri was a small freighter of 4200 tons. She had no passenger accommodation, and carried a mixed cargo from London, calling at Swansea, to Baltimore. On the return trip she carried mainly cattle, with some grain and flour. No doubt the Swansea connection had attracted Loftus to this line. Missouri was, in her chief officer's words, 'a snug little ship'.

On her second voyage across the Atlantic she left London on the 28th March 1889 with a crew of 27. In command was Captain Hamilton Murrell. The chief officer was Thomas Gates who became a life-long friend of Loftus, and ended a distinguished career as commodore of the Atlantic service after 45 years in command. The other two executive officers were a man named Forsyth and Loftus. For this voyage the Missouri had a full cargo of mixed freight in her holds, and the 'tween decks filled with bales of wool and rags. The usual call at Swansea was omitted. On 5th April, when the ship was in mid-Atlantic some 500 miles east of Newfoundland, Loftus was officer of the watch when at 1.15 pm he sighted a steamer off the port bow flying distress signals. She was the SS Danmark, a Danish emigrant ship bound for the United States with 664 passengers and a crew of 69. Her propeller shaft had broken tearing a hole in her plating and she lay helpless in a rough sea with five feet of water in her hold. Captain Murrell's first plan was to tow the disabled ship to St John's in Newfoundland. Towing began by nightfall but wind and sea were rising and the strain was great, lifting the Missouri's deck beams under the towing bitts. At first light the look-out reported ice ahead. The Captain and officers were agreed that towing through ice would be out of the question; and Captain Murrell decided to alter course and make for the Azores 800 miles to the south east. But at 9.00 am the Danmark signalled 'Am sinking. Take our people off.' Her chief officer came aboard the Missouri and reported that the water was gaining on the pumps and it seemed unlikely that the ship would remain afloat much longer.

Captain Murrell and his officers were now faced with a formidable problem. On board the sinking ship were 22 babies of one year or under, 65 children under 11, 200 women and 446 men, in addition to the crew of 69. There was a strong wind and a rough sea, and the Missouri could not safely keep closer to the disabled vessel than about a quarter mile. The only means of access to the Missouri were rope ladders hung over the side. Although she had neither food nor accommodation the Missouri had plenty of fresh water from her steam condensers. There were nine lifeboats — rowing boats — two from the Missouri and the rest from the Danmark, each of which could take about 20 people at a time.

Gates was put in charge of the reception arrangements, and Forsyth and Loftus each took charge of a lifeboat. Luckily the Danmark had aboard a party of Lake Michigan fishermen returning from a holiday in their native country, who were skilled in the management of small boats, and they took charge of the lifeboats from the Danmark. The smallest of the boats was used solely for transferring food. The babies and infants were put on the first lifeboat to leave, accompanied by two of the mothers. Meanwhile the Chief Officer's party was busy throwing the 'tween deck cargo overboard. Wicker coaling baskets, slung on ropes, were got ready for hauling up babies. Gates described the scene:

> When the first boatload of women arrived alongside the Missouri, another problem developed when it was found that owing to the rolling of the ship they could not climb the rope ladders let down to them. The first woman to try it was submerged in a wave. Orders were then passed by myself — for I had charge of hoisting the infants — to sling the women in ropes, and this was done by slipping a running bowline over the woman's shoulders, and heaving her up like a sack of potatoes. It was a rough method but it worked and in a short time we had all the mothers on board. They rushed at once to their little ones, who had been deposited by the sailors on the saloon floor. There they were rolling round in rather lively fashion, all crying at

once. But not one had been injured, and all were soon set
to rights by their mothers . . . The waves were rolling so
high at the time that for a moment all the boats were
hidden from view of the Missouri's deck. This must have
been quite terrifying to people not familiar with the sea.

The work went on all day, and at 4.50 pm the commander of the
Danmark, Captain Knudsen, went over the side into the last boat.
The rescue had been effected without loss of life or serious injury
to anyone; although the unfortunate second officer Forsyth had
several teeth knocked out in a minor collision of his boat with the
side of the Danmark. At the end of the day all the boats had
suffered damage and were cast adrift except the boat of which
Loftus had been in charge – a tribute to the seamanship which he
had learnt on the Conway. He recalls that one of the passengers in
his boat that day was a blind old lady of 87.

That night there was a rising gale and a high sea, sending solid
water over the crowded ship. The men were mainly on deck, the
women and children stowed into every cabin and corner that could
be found. There were twelve girls in the wheelhouse; the
engineer's storeroom was crowded with women. The Chief
Officer's cabin became a labour ward, and at 1.00 am a new voice
was added to the ship's complement. Little Atlanta Missourie, as
she was later christened, was clothed in an outfit cut from some of
the officers' shirts. The emigrants had a wretched night; exhausted, hungry, soaked to the skin, they had lost all their money
and possessions. The children wailed miserably. But by 8.30 am
the steward, a man of great resource, had provided everyone in
the ship with breakfast of a sort; with boiled rice and condensed
milk for the children. By midday the gale abated a little and the
ship was hove to, head to the sea, to give people a chance to dry
out. Next day there were calm seas, and the sun came out.
Hogsheads were cut in half to make tubs, to which bars of soap
were attached by lanyards. 'Everybody had a good fresh water
scrub and after that they all felt much better.' On the afternoon of
the third day the Azores were sighted, and after a night of fog the
ship was off the little port of Punta Delgada. The pilot who came
alongside was astonished at what he saw.

Meanwhile fears were being expressed in Britain and America
over the fate of the two vessels, both of which were overdue. One
of the waterlogged lifeboats of the Danmark had been sighted.
Despite their safe arrival in the Azores there was still no means of

communicating with the outside world except by boat. Captain Murrell acted with great energy and resource. It was decided to take all the women and children and families to Philadelphia on the Missouri, leaving 370 men to be fetched later. Within two days all necessary provisions had been bought, Captain Murrell going up into the mountains to select bullocks and sheep for slaughtering; the ship had been cleansed; cloth purchased and made into mattresses filled with heather; canvas rooms built for the women and children in the 'tween decks; wash houses and sanitary arrangements completed; and a whole variety of stores purchased from the island's primitive resources, including sweets for the children. The voyage to Philadelphia lasted ten days during which time the women made clothes for themselves and their children from a quantity of calico which the Captain had bought. There was only one pair of scissors, which was tied to the door of the chartroom.

The arrival of the Missouri in the United States and the story of the rescue became the sensation of the year.

> Press and public went wild over the rescue. Honours were showered on Captain Murrell, his officers and all hands. We were given illuminated addresses and medals and gold watches and what not; and were talked to and praised until there seemed no end to it. After being heaped with honours at Philadelphia we went to Baltimore and had it all over again. There were public receptions at Cardiff, Swansea and Colchester. In London we were received at the Mansion House where the officers were given gold watches, and cheques for two months' pay were given to all hands. The King of Denmark knighted Captain Murrell with the Order of Dannebrog, and Prince Bismark of Germany sent his congratulations.

The officers sat for their portraits to the artist Thomas Hemy, who painted a graphic picture of the rescue entitled 'And Every Soul Was Saved.' This painting in which Loftus is shown in the bows of the second lifeboat handling a rope (Forsyth's boat is in the foreground, and Gates is on deck next to the Captain) went on public exhibition in various towns including Swansea, where it was shown at 98 Oxford Street. There was an admission charge of sixpence. The picture frame was made of rope hawser the same size as that used by the Missouri during the tow. A copy of the painting in a gilt frame of similar design was presented to each of the officers. Gifts to Captain Murrell included three gold medals,

two gold watches and eleven illuminated addresses. A Mr J.
Dunbar Hylton of New Jersey gave the Captain five volumes of his
own poetry. Loftus received gold medals from the citizens of
Philadelphia and the Life Saving Benevolent Institution of New
York, and a gold watch from the Lord Mayor of London. He
particularly treasured a posy of sea pinks picked by Sam Richards
on the Rhosili cliffs and presented to him to mark the occasion.

On her return voyage across the Atlantic the Missouri carried, in
addition to a general cargo, 494 bullocks, and three thoroughbred
horses one of them a blood American trotter. It pleased Loftus very
much to discover that the horses belonged to one of Lady
Llanover's grandsons, Mr Herbert of Llanarth who had been on a
diplomatic mission in Washington, and he enjoyed chatting with the
groom about Llanover.

Swansea, as we saw, was a regular port of call for the Missouri.
With the fame of the rescue there were plenty of visitors wanting to
see the ship when she next docked there. A few months after the
rescue Loftus wrote from Swansea docks, after a brief visit from his
father.

I was so glad to hear that you got home in such good case,
dear Father, 3 hours and 25 mins, wonderfully good time.
Yes indeed we had a most jolly and long-to-be-remembered
afternoon; you can hardly imagine the pleasure it was to
me even being able to pat dear old Darkie again . . . Well,
I have had 9 visitors today, they were as follows: First
George Richards, secondly Morgan Beynon, his
brother-in-law, Captain Grove and Captain Chalk. Thirdly,
'our' William Beynon, and lastly the Rev Clark (I think of
the Grammar School), Gwyn Jones (an old Llandovery
boy), his curate, and one of the masters of the Grammar
School. I was most glad to see George Richards and W.
Beynon. They seemed so very 'homeified'. Good George
Richards came on board in the most businesslike manner,
with his stick and the basket of grapes. I made him sit
down in my cabin and afterwards showed him over the
ship.
  W. Beynon was on board for some time. I should be
afraid to say how many times he or G. Richards said 'Well!
Well!! Well!!!'. What would they say if they saw the
Arcadia! I will try to find a nice church in America, dear
Mother. Those new stirrups awfully grand, dear Father. Do
make Beynon keep Darkie's heels close clipped. I think
you must see what a wonderful difference it makes in his
appearance.

Calls at Swansea sometimes gave Loftus an opportunity for a few days at home, followed by a last view of the Rectory as the *Missouri* sailed down channel:

> I consider that four days holiday about the jolliest I ever spent. Add to dear C.'s list (1) Service at Rhos church (2) the pleasure of getting Darkie ready and 'sending' you to Llangennith church, dear Father (3) tennis at Hillend (4) not only the drive but the excursion to Pennard. I actually got a splendid view of the house as we passed after leaving Swansea that morning. The fact of my seeing it so well was due to Capt Bocquet steering a more northerly course than Murrell is in the habit of doing, and the morning was a beautifully clear one. You can fancy my delight as Rhosili Point slowly receded, inch by inch, and the dear old place, first the potato field, then the house itself, and then the barn, came slowly into view.

Captain Loftus Lucas in 1918.

Promotion for Loftus came quickly, and after short spells as second officer of the Maine and the Mississippi, he was appointed chief officer in March 1892, immediately after passing his final Board of Trade examination. His Master's Certificate, issued in March of that year, was what was known as a 'square rigged ticket' qualifying the holder to take command of either a sailing ship or a steamer. Then followed four years as chief officer during which he served on three of the Company's ships, the Maine, the Michigan and the Mississippi, before being given command, in May 1896, of the Minnesota, a sister ship of the Missouri.

10

1890–98
The Last Years at Rhosili

It was during the 1880s that the Rector bought a horse, Darkie by name, often mentioned in Loftus's letters home, and the trap, which was kept in one of George Thomas's barns. Hitherto he had done his parish work on foot. The family were all strong walkers. They had to be. On more than one occasion Loftus, returning from a voyage, would arrive at Swansea High Street station about 4 am, and set off at once to walk the 18 miles to Rhosili. He would go by

Tottenham on Darkie, Rhosili Sands, 1890.

the red road over Cefn Bryn; and then from Llanddewi corner along the lane past old Hentlas and so to the top of Rhosili Down, arriving at the Rectory in good time for breakfast. Darkie had trouble with his feet, and the Rector sold him in the 1890s, and once more took to walking about west Gower. At the age of 74 he walked from the Rectory to Penmaen for a meeting and back again.

It was on horseback, however, that the Rector is remembered by some, from hearing their parents speak of him. In their minds' eye they see, riding slowly by, a heavily built man of austere appearance, dressed in a black frock coat and top hat. Not many people came close enough to him to observe that there was often a twinkle in his eye. When he had Darkie it was his habit to ride over to Llangennith on Sunday to take the service. Dismounting at the churchyard. The congregation waited respectfully inside the to robe in the vestry, and advance up the nave 'at a brisk trot'. It was said that his sermons were short and pithy. At the end of the service there were no handshakes in the porch, no chatting in the churchyard. The congregation wiated respectfully inside the church until the Rector had departed. Fortunately Rebecca had just that gift of approachability, a way of getting on well with people, which her husband so conspicuously lacked. She was a tireless parish worker with a fund of strong practical common-sense. People confided their troubles to her, and sought her advice on the naming of infants and the treatment of ailments. Her musical gifts enabled her to train Rhosili church choir with authority. She ran a successful Sunday school; and under her quiet influence some who had deserted the church for the chapel came back again into the church.

In the 1880s it was decided that Rhosili church would have to be thoroughly restored. As we saw in Chapter 5 some essential work had been done soon after the Rector arrived in Rhosili but further restoration was prevented by lack of funds. Now, for Rhosili and other south Gower churches, a formidable benefactor appeared on the scene in the person of Miss Emily Talbot of Penrice Castle. She was a granddaughter of the Thomas Mansel Talbot whom we met in Chapter 3. Her father. C. R. M. Talbot, one of the dominant figures in 19th century Glamorgan, lived at Margam Castle, leaving Penrice to his unmarried daughters Emily and Olive. Of the two sisters Emily seems to have been the dominant character. A large proportion, perhaps the majority, of the inhabitants of south-west Gower were her tenants, and towards them she became a benevolent autocrat combining in herself the functions of a Housing, Welfare and Education authority. She was a vigorous upholder of the established church. In later life it became her habit to give an annual tea party at Penrice for the children of the neighbourhood, at which there were presents for all. It was noticed however by the chapel children that it was the children from the church families who always seemed to get the best presents. At Rhosili, Rebecca was the intermediary through whom Miss Talbot's directives to the village were issued:

> Dear Mrs Lucas,
> The case of John Morris is certainly rather a difficult one. The old man would certainly be better in the Union, as you say he has no one to take care of him. Do you think you could persuade him to go in? If not I am willing to give him the 2/– a week . . .

> Dear Mrs Lucas,
> I have been making enquiries about Mrs Williams and yesterday saw the cottage, though she was away. It is a wretched little place and very insanitary. I should like to pull it down but unfortunately it is let with the farm to the Beynons and as long as they keep the farm I cannot very well interfere. Mrs Beynon told me she wanted it for her invalid daughter but I am quite sure no invalid ought to go there. Mrs Beynon seems to be such a loud tongued woman that she is not easy to talk to — but I have asked Wilson to see if he can do any thing with her.
> I am thinking whether it would be possible to build a Sunday School and a parish room combined at Rhosili. In many places a reading room in winter is very popular. This would take in Dissenters as well as Churchmen and would have to be managed by a Committee . . . I was very sorry not to see you yesterday but it was too far to walk to your house . . .

> Dear Mrs Lucas,
> . . . I have given Mr Nicholl instructions to build a room for the Sunday School at Rhosili, but I think the proposed reading room must be given up for the present. The people do not seem inclined to do the haulage, and I fear the reading room would not be a success unless Rhosili and Middleton and the whole Parish would join in it . . . There is at present a good deal of quarrelling going on in the Parish and so I fear there would be no chance of their combining in the way they should do to make the room a success . . .

Dear Mrs Lucas,

I send a small pattern of the apron some of us are going to wear at the Bazaar. It should be made of muslin and insertion and the whole apron should be edged with lace, all the way round. I think you can get the lace from 4d to 6d the yard. We all intend wearing a red rosette. This will indicate we are officials and enable us to pass in and out of the Bazaar . . . I dare say you and Mr Lucas will come over in the morning, for tho' the Bazaar does not open till one o'clock we shall be some time arranging the stall. . .

Dear Mrs. Lucas,

The day is so unfortunately wet that I am afraid I shall not be able to go to Rhosili today. But if it clears at all I will certainly go. I have sent over the things and if it does not clear perhaps you would find it possible to put (the children's tea) off till tomorrow. I am afraid I could not be present either on Wednesday or the next day . . . I am so sorry as I know the children like to see me. There is a list of the things sent and I have sent five shillings worth of pence . . .

Dear Mrs Lucas,

I am so very sorry we shall not be able to go to the tea tomorrow. I have been very poorly the last few days and we have just discovered that the drainage here is in a very bad state, so my Doctor has ordered me off at once, and we are going to Margam tomorrow. I can't say how vexed I am but I really dare not stay here. I will send over all the things as usual with the still-room maid and will you kindly give the women who help whatever you think right from the money you have of mine. I do not want any buns returned (if there should be too many). Perhaps you would give them to anyone in the Parish who would like them . . . I will tell the still-room maid to ask you for orders.

Dear Mrs Lucas,

I shall be very willing to give £450 towards the restoration of Rhosili church but I must decline to sign the bond. I have therefore returned it. Between the money you have already collected and the money I now promise the *money* difficulty will be overcome and I hope the restoration will proceed. I am sorry there has been so much delay in sending the rewards for the Sunday School girls . . .

The restoration did proceed. The church was re-roofed; a new porch built; pulpit, lectern, choir stalls and pitch pine seats for the congregation installed. The altar rail was erected, the floors tiled and the accumulated soil finally removed from the walls and the base of the Norman doorway. A vestry was made below the tower, and a heating stove put in. While all this was going on the church services were held in the Board school room at Middleton. A few old features such as the stone bench table behind the new altar — presented by Miss Talbot — were lost but great care was taken to preserve the character of the church, which was reopened in June 1891. The cost of the work was £874–2–0 of which Miss Talbot subscribed £550. Village efforts — collections, teas and concerts — produced £130, and the rest came in donations ranging from five guineas downwards. Mr Rosser of Reynoldston was the builder and the architect was Mr Ewen Christian, a well-known restorer of churches in Victorian times. Neither Rebecca nor Miss Talbot was able to make much headway against this masterful character. Miss Talbot intended to supervise the design of the church fittings, but on hearing of this Mr Christian wrote to the Rector:

> With regard to the pulpit, lectern and prayer desk Mr Christian *begs* that Miss Talbot will kindly allow him to design them so as to be in harmony with the rest of the work. Kindly press this if you can as it is so very unsatisfactory to have things which are incongruous placed in the church, and to get the credit of them afterwards.

Christian won his point, and Miss Talbot had to be content with designing the altar cloth. Rebecca was rash enough to complain that a chimney would look rather odd, sticking up out of the roof of the tower. This drew a crushing rebuke:

> I am sorry that you are so troubled about our chimney. People are very unreasonable about church chimneys. They will have stoves and warmth but want the chimneys hidden away, the consequence of which is that the fires will not draw, the church is filled with smoke and everything is spoilt and uncomfortable . . . There is no patent way of making a stove consume its own smoke without a chimney. The only substitute for a chimney is a pipe through the roof and this, besides being highly dangerous, is ten times more shocking than any chimney can be — only people have got used to hideous and unsafe stove pipes, and are not used to honest chimneys.

With Rebecca routed over the chimney, the Rector's wish to have the inside of the porch plastered was easily dealt with:

> Plaster is not very nice in the Porch. It gets damp and dirty, and young men and boys are very apt to scribble upon and deface it, being out of sight when the church

door is shut.

When all had been accomplished the Church was reopened with a grand day of ceremonial, in the presence of the Bishop of St Davids and many of the Gower clergy. There were three services held, all of them crowded. The Rector entertained the visiting dignitaries to lunch, and there was a public tea for the village, in a marquee. The church also had a new harmonium, described as 'an admirable and costly instrument'. It was played by Tottenham who demonstrated its capabilities 'in a masterly fashion'. Among the individual fund raising efforts was a poem written by Loftus entitled 'Rhossili Church'. It was printed and sold for a penny a copy, realising £1–2–9. 'Very pretty and describes the place well' was Miss Talbot's verdict.

During the 1870s came the first stirrings of what was to become, eventually, the Gower tourist trade. At Easter, and again in July and August, a few discerning middle-class families began to find in Gower sea air and solitude amid a land and seascape of rare quality. By horse bus, and in hired breaks, and towards the end of the century on bicycles, came the first of the few. They discovered the few inns and cottages prepared to take visitors and vanished happily on to the cliffs and commons and sandy bays. It is difficult to convey to a modern visitor the remoteness of Gower in the late 19th and early 20th centuries. As late as the 1920s you could walk in August — we did it — from Rhosili village across the sands to the Burry Holmes and back again without meeting a single soul. In the 1930s it was still rare to see anyone on the Gower cliffs; and on our many pilgrimages to the Worm's Head I do not recollect sharing our solitude with a living creature except the sea birds and the seals, a few sheep on the Inner Head, and the strange and beautiful inhabitants of the rock pools.

Some time between 1878 and 1885 William Richards and his wife built a cottage, which they called Worm's Head Cottage, on the edge of the cliff beyond Harepits. Here they offered board and lodging for holidaymakers. There were plenty of vacant sites and empty cottages in Gower in those days and I can only suppose that the Richards chose a site so mercilessly exposed to the winter gales on account of the breathtaking view of Rhosili Bay which it would afford for the visitors in summer. During the summer of 1889 a party of five arrived at Worm's Head Cottage, having walked along the cliffs from their lodgings in Porteynon. They were Mrs Annette

Cunnington, a widow in her early 40s, and her children Annette (known as Tiny) aged 15, Val (13), Robin (12) and Will (11). They were so thrilled by this their first sight of Worm's Head and Rhosili that they at once booked the rooms in the cottage for the following year. During the next ten years the Cunningtons spent several of their summer holidays at Worm's Head Cottage. It was stone built in the traditional Gower style, whitewashed, with sash windows, a porch and a slate roof. Will Cunnington reminds us that there was an earth closet in the garden; windows which opened but a couple of inches; you washed, if at all, in cold water; and the beds were as hard as granite. When I first stayed there in 1926 it was exactly the same, except that Mr and Mrs Richards were replaced by Mr and Mrs Thomas.

Mrs Cunnington was one of the 14 daughters of Robert Valentine Leach of Devizes Castle in Wiltshire. Leach started life as a corn merchant in Devizes. When his business failed he moved to South Wales. Here he acquired Vernon House, a mansion on the banks of the River Neath at Briton Ferry. He ran it as a private lunatic asylum from 1843 to 1860, employing a Dr Pigg as his resident medical officer. When Charles Pigg fell in love with Kate, one of Leach's numerous daughters, his prospective father-in-law consented to the match provided, so it is said, he was not compelled to have a Pigg for a son-in-law. The Doctor changed his name to Pegge, and they were married in 1861. There was money to be made in South Wales in those days, and Leach made a fortune, not so much from the asylum as from successful ventures into the tin-plate industry. On his return to Devizes in 1860 he paid off his old creditors and completed the rebuilding of the ancient Norman castle in a Victorian Baronial style. He also acquired a villa at Bordighera on the Italian Riviera, where he and his family would spend the winter months. Annette, his favourite daughter, married Alfred Cunnington, a member of a well-known Devizes family who owned a wine merchants' business in the town, and many of whom were noted as antiquaries and archaeologists. Alfred, a brilliantly able young man, an amateur scientist who built the first telephone ever put to practical use in England — it ran from the Cunnington's home to their office in Devizes — died of typhoid fever in 1879 at the age of 29. Annette moved to Clifton where her sons were educated at the College, and Tiny her daughter at the Girls' High School. Meanwhile Charles and Kate Pegge continued to run the asylum at Vernon House.

Many of these Cunningtons, Leaches and Pegges came to know Rhosili well. Mrs Annette Cunnington and her children led the way there, and were a noticeable addition to the congregation in Rhosili church on Sunday mornings. It is not surprising that one day an invitation arrived at Worm's Head Cottage for the family to call and take tea at the Rectory. This was, I think, in the summer of 1892, when Tiny was a few months short of her 18th birthday. The boys managed to find a good excuse for avoiding the tea-party — perhaps the tide was just right for bass fishing off the rocks — and Annette and Tiny set off on their own, along the lane past George Thomas's farmyard. They wore ankle length skirts and carried walking sticks, and picked their way carefully round the muddy pools beyond the rocket house and on to the Rectory path. Tiny had just left school at the end of the summer term. She was short and dark with a neat figure, a face of classic beauty, and a gentle and serene expression in her dark eyes which any young man would have found devastating. Tiny was not particularly looking forward to the tea party. She was shy with strangers, and the Rector, from what little she had seen of him, seemed a severe and formidable sort of man.

The two ladies had not got very far along the steep side of Rhosili Down when they saw a young man leave the Rectory and come along the path towards them. He was fair haired and noticeably good looking, and as he came nearer Tiny observed that although he strode easily and strongly along the rough path his gait had a slight limp. This was Loftus, come to show them the way. They learnt that he had just come home on leave from his ship the SS Maine on which he was the chief officer. The Rector told them with some pride that his son had recently gained his master's certificate and was hoping to have command of his own ship before long. Loftus made himself most charming and agreeable to both Annette and Tiny who enjoyed the tea-party more than they had expected. The Rector turned out to be much less formidable than he had first appeared, telling little jokes and stories to amuse his guests.

Less than two years after this meeting at Rhosili Rectory, Loftus and Tiny sought their parents' consent for them to marry. The Rector and Rebecca were delighted. 'A marriage made in Heaven', wrote the Rector with enthusiasm. Annette on the other hand was dismayed. The young people had had little more than a holiday acquaintance. Tiny was only 19. The thought of losing her daughter to a man she hardly knew and who was likely to spend most of his life on the high seas was more than she could bear, and revived in all its bitterness her own tragedy, the death of an adored husband after pitifully few years of happiness. Loftus and Tiny had to wait three years before being married. Annette had a high opinion of her prospective son-in-law, but she could not conquer her misgivings about Tiny marrying a sailor. The marriage was delayed in the hopes that Loftus might be able to find a job on shore, but this came to nothing. Loftus took command of the Minnesota in 1896, and on the 20th May 1897 he and Tiny were married in the Church of St Mary the Less in Cambridge.

During the 1880s and 1890s Rebecca spent much time organising evening concerts, held in the Board Schoolroom at Middleton, in aid of Church restoration. The performers were principally the Rector's family and friends. The programme for 21st August 1895 was typical, and shows the kind of music which people liked to hear, or which they enjoyed playing and singing in the 1890s:

(Left to right) Tottenham, Loftus, Flora, Caroline and Rebecca, c.1893.

PART I.

1. SOLO AND CHORUS — The Gipsies' Tent .... *T. Cooke*

2. PIANO DUETS — Danse Orientale
   Danse Hindoue .... *Chaminade*
   Miss M. and Mr. P. T. LUCAS

3. SONG — Beauty's Eyes .... *Tosti*
   Mr. C. H. SOUTHEY

4. SONG — Wiegenlied .... *Brahms*
   Miss FLORA LUCAS

5. WHISTLING SOLO — Valse from Romeo et Juliette .... *Gounod*
   Mr. ERNEST HELME

6. SONG — Going to Market .... *Diehl*
   Miss SOUTHEY

7. PIANO SOLO — Caprice Espagnol .... *Moszkowski*
   Mrs. SOUTHEY

8. RECITATION — The Angel's Passion .... *C. H. Southey*
   Mr. C. H. SOUTHEY

9. PIANO DUET — Fairy Queen .... *S. Smith*
   Miss CUNNINGTON and Mr. P. T. LUCAS

10. VOCAL DUET — Blow, Gentle Wind .... *Myles B. Foster*
    Miss FLORA LUCAS and Miss LOIS BEYNON

INTERVAL OF TEN MINUTES

PART II

1. VOCAL DUET — I would that my Love .... *Mendelssohn*
   Miss SOUTHEY and Mr. C. H. SOUTHEY

2. VIOLIN SOLO — We're a' NODDIN .... *J. Bêrotte*
   Miss LUCAS

3. SONG — O'er Life's Dark Sea .... *P. T. Lucas*
   Miss LOIS BEYNON

4. PIANO SOLO — Mazurek .... *Paderewski*
   La Capricieuse .... *Heller*
   Mr. P. T. LUCAS

5. SONG — The Promise of Life .... *Cowen*
   Miss SOUTHEY

6. VOCAL TRIO — Three Little Maids .... *Sullivan*
   *Miss FLORA LUCAS, Miss OLIVE BEVAN and
   Miss LOIS BEYNON*

7. WHISTLING SOLO ....
   Mr. ERNEST HELME

8. SONG — Madchens Wunsch .... *Chopin*
   Miss FLORA LUCAS

9. PIANO DUET — Qui Vive .... *W. Ganz*
   Miss M. LUCAS and Miss CUNNINGTON

10. COMIC SONG — The First Cigar .... *Corney Grain*
    Mr. P. T. LUCAS

GOD SAVE THE QUEEN

The programme gives an opportunity to say something about the performers. Caroline, the Rector's eldest daughter who played the violin solo, was now 24, taking occasional posts as a *Lady's Companion*. She had no particular qualifications and suffered from poor health. There were a great many girls of Caroline's social class seeking jobs as 'companions' in the 1890s, and posts were hard to find. In the winter of 1897/8 Caroline tried a job as a 'Lady Cook' but it involved more than cooking and Caroline left. She wrote to her parents: 'I expect you were not surprised to hear about my leaving Mrs Baines. It is strange that people can expect ladies to go and work for them as kitchen maids'. The Rector commented: 'Strange they should ask a Lady also to do the scullery duties, washing up all crockery, saucepans etc. I suppose the idea is to free the Lady herself from the presence of a common maidservant. Well,' he concluded, 'another bubble burst . . . the idea of a young Lady acting as lady cook plus as kitchen maid. I imagine the term "lady cook" was never heard of until end of 19th C.' On another occasion when Caroline went for interview she found she would be expected to perform services for her employer of horrifying intimacy. The Rector was left almost speechless. 'Enough to take one's breath away,' he wrote, 'Fancy the creature talking of her legs being like a baby's legs! And as to the bath business I do really think Caroline would have sooner died than accede to such a thing; inconceivably dreadful.' The 'bath business' may have been a little dubious; but the refusal to wash up is a reminder of the traditional conventions and class distinctions which no doubt seemed entirely normal at the time. At Rhosili Rectory, although money was tight, Rebecca always had a maid and, when the children were babies, a nurse as well.

Both May and Flora were, like Caroline, rather at a loose end in 1895. They both had excellent school records, but they lived in a world where work as a companion or governess was almost the only alternative to marriage: and how could they ever go about in the world of middle-class society and meet marriageable young men when they had no money — and at Rhosili Rectory of all places. Flora had just left school, and in the autumn went for a time as paying guest in the family of a Pastor at Hamburg, where she had the companionship of the Pastor's daughter Hette, a girl of her own age, and took lessons in German and singing. The Rector was a believer in the value of foreign travel for young people, and he willingly scraped to find the boarding fees for Flora. But she had no spending money, and felt lonely and isolated at Hamburg.

> It is bitterly cold today. Our bedroom window is all frozen
> over in the most lovely patterns, like ferns and
> seaweed . . . I am reduced to a state of poverty now, for of
> the ten shillings I have to pay back six shillings that they
> lent me. Couldn't you sell something of mine and send me
> the money? Isn't there a seal or a fan that belongs to me?
> It is miserable not to have enough money and I know *you*
> can't send me any more — and what do I want with a seal
> and a fan?

Returning to the concert programme, where we find Flora singing and May playing the piano, I see that Tiny played two piano duets. She was a good pianist, but hated appearing on any sort of public platform and I doubt whether, even for Loftus's sake, she could have been prevailed upon to play solo. Olive Bevan and Lois Beynon were in the church choir. Lois had a very good voice. She was the daughter of William Beynon who kept the Ship Inn at Middleton (not the same Beynons who live there today). She later married Petty Officer Edgar Evans RN, a Rhosili man who died on the journey back from the South Pole with Captain Scott in 1912.

Ernest Helme, billed in the programme for his whistling solos, was to acquire a great reputation in Gower as a musician and trainer of choirs, and he was the moving spirit of the Gower eisteddfod in the years before the first world war. When the world famous coloratura singer Dame Adelina Patti came to live at Craig-y-nos in the upper Swansea valley, Ernest Helme would accompany her at the piano in charity concerts. At the end of the performance she would introduce Ernest as one 'who can whistle my songs as well as I can sing them'. This he would then proceed to do. He was a man of considerable charm, and he and his mother were close friends of the Lucases. He was thought at one time to be keen on May, but he was a good deal younger than she was, and nothing ever came of it.

Tottenham's contribution to the concert must have been of high quality. He had left Llandovery school in 1888 with an exhibition

May Lucas at Rhosili Rectory, 1897.

in classics to Oriel College, Oxford. Here he read 'greats' (classics and philosophy) and took his degree in 1892. After some early tutoring and teaching jobs he was appointed in the summer of 1895 as master in charge of music, and to teach classics, at Yarlet Hall, a boys' preparatory school near Stafford. He was already an accomplished musician and composer who had published several works. His best known composition was his setting of the *Benedicite,* of which Novello's sold some 22 000 copies during his lifetime. Other compositions of his early days were a cantata for treble voices in twelve parts, and a trio for harp, violin and cello. He was also an excellent exponent of the art of the Comic Song, so much enjoyed at Victorian and Edwardian musical evenings.

Sam Bevan 'The Post' at Rhosili Rectory in the 1890s. This and the other local portraits were taken by Tottenham Lucas with his small Kodak camera which produced 1¾″ x 1¼″ prints.

Last the Southeys, whose names figure so prominently in this programme. Charles Southey came to live at Rhosili in the summer of 1894. He was the grandson of Robert Southey the well-known poet and man of letters. His father, the Reverend Cuthbert Southey, younger son of the poet, was Vicar of Askham near Penrith in the Lake District. Charles was himself an aspiring poet, had a charming tenor voice, and was undoubtedly rather odd. He furnished 'the cave on the Worm's Head' with a table and chair and used to retire there to write poetry, claiming that it was 'magnificent in a gale'. There was a precedent for this kind of thing. On the other side of the Bristol Channel, on the north Cornish coast, Parson Hawker of Morwenstow who died in 1875 had built for himself out of driftwood a hut on the face of a precipitous sea cliff where he too retired to write poetry. Hawker's hut is still there, but where is Southey's cave? There is indeed a cave on the Worm's Head, facing west at the extreme end of the outer head, some way above high water mark, but it is only accessible by rock scrambling and its floor is far too rough for any kind of furniture. The middle head has a charming archway in its northern face with a flat floor and a grand view across Rhosili bay, but it is a wind funnel and tables or chairs would be quickly blown out to sea in any sort of a gale. The most likely site for Southey's cave is on the inner head where, Kit Morgan tells us in his *Wanderings in Gower* first published in the 1860s, there was 'an artificial cave (smugglers') well known in days of yore but now overgrown with briars and thorns'. This cave no longer exists. Very likely it collapsed with the erosion of the sandy cliff on the south side of the inner head.

Southey was well received at the Rectory. He and Tottenham seem to have taken to each other, and entered on a musical collaboration. Together they published *Evening Song. The words by Charles H. Southey. The music by P. Tottenham Lucas. Published by the Orpheus Music Publishing Co. of London and Toronto*. Meanwhile strange rumours about Southey began to circulate. He had a passion for revolver shooting, and had been seen fingering his gun in church; he had shot a donkey and a valuable sheep dog, slipping a £5 note under the farmer's door in recompense; some boys camping in a tent in Mewslade had found themselves the centre of target practice and had legged it for home. Then Southey disappeared from his lodgings in Rhosili, and later reappeared with a girl in church on Sunday. The Rector wrote to Loftus:

> . . . he asked your mother to call on her which she did yesterday with the girls and asked them both to take tea here tomorrow. She is tolerable looking, nothing at all striking, yellow hair, black eyebrows; said to be 19 but looks older. *Never* heard of a similar case; a girl coming so far across country with a gentleman. Mr S. says they are engaged. She has lodgings at Harepits. He of course remains in his house, but they are always walking and poking about together. Gower people will not spare them as to remarks etc . . .

Southey and the young lady were married shortly afterwards and joined by Southey's sister they took a prominent part in the concert. It is a pity that the text of Southey's poem *The Angel's Passion* has not come to light. It sounds overcharged with emotion, perhaps as a result of having been composed in a gale on the Worm's Head. It was not long after this concert that Southey again vanished from Rhosili — this time for good and leaving his wife behind him. The Rector at first took a fairly charitable view.

> . . . poor man he does not evidently possess the amount of

sense that all people except idiots have; it seems Mrs S's
father lately died, whereupon he expected to come into a
good fortune (which would have all been spent in a couple
of years) but I understand he finds it is very properly 'tied
up' so that he and his wife can only get the income of it. At
this, so the gossips say, he is not a little disgusted . . .

It later transpired that Southey in fact had stolen all of his wife's
money that he could get his hands on. The reaction at the Rectory
can be imagined; particularly when Rebecca, not long afterwards
received the following letter:

Dear Mrs Lucas,
    No doubt you will be astonished at a letter from me,
who you all doubtless regard as being beyond all chance of
reformation. Well I think of coming down to Oxwich for a
time, or Rhosili. My sister is shortly going out to South
Africa. She is to be married shortly. I am going to ask a
most extraordinary favour of you. Will you — can you —
would you — like to take her for a week or ten days. I will
make it all right regarding — you understand. I should like
her to be at Rhosili once more with me before we part
perhaps for ever. I enclose her last photo. Please return it.
She *has* changed; and her voice is glorious. She does not
know I am writing this. I inclose her address. Please forgive
anything you may dislike in this letter and believe me yours
very sincerely C. H. Southey
    Accept this vol with my very kind regards.

The 'vol' enclosed with Southey's letter was a delightful edition
of the *New Testament* in Greek, published by the Clarendon Press
in 1828, bound in red leather, tooled in gold. Rebecca gave it to
Tottenham. Where did Southey get it from? I like to think that I
may have in my possession a book from his grandfather Robert
Southey's famous library. Southey's story ends with a newspaper
cutting, undated:

At Shap, Westmoreland, yesterday, Charles Southey, son
of the late vicar of Askham and grandson of the poet
Robert Southey was sent to gaol for a week for begging at
Patterdale Hall on Sunday night. He told the Bench a
pathetic story. His father, he said, gave him a good
education, but no trade, so he took up literature. He got
married and had a comfortable home, but his wife left him
years ago and he had to sell his home. Afterwards he stole
half a sovereign, for which he was sent to prison. He had
since been unable to pursue literary work, his appearance
being against him. 'I have not known what it is to have a

proper meal for a long time' added the prisoner, 'but have
had to subsist at the best of times on fish and chips in
common lodging houses'.

Southey might perhaps have added in mitigation that there was
a history of mental instability in the family. I think Rebecca may
have had a soft spot for Southey, with his love of music and
charming tenor voice. She pinned the cutting about him to a sheet
of paper on which she had copied out a story about a tramp who
redeemed his past failings by loyal work as a gardener. Rebecca
was always practical and this was the kind of path to redemption
which would have appealed to her.

Loftus and Tiny were now living in West Hampstead, conveniently placed for Loftus's ship, the Minnesota, plying between
London and New York. Tiny did accompany Loftus on at least one
voyage across the Atlantic, but she was desperately seasick and
scarcely able to leave her cabin. Charles was also in Hampstead,
living with his Aunt Yetta. The Rector kept them up to date with
snippets of Gower news.

Rhos Rectory 11/2/98

My dear Loftus
   Your last letter also one from off Dover came all
right . . . I cannot help thinking you had a much better
passage out this time at all events. The spell of gales here
over for the present. Marvellous winter here! I never
remember such — not an atom of frost or snow. Last
Sunday as I issued from the back gate for Rhosili service,
coming down Rolling Tor for a long way on the path I to
my infinite astonishment saw an *immense crowd,* a long
procession of people coming along. I could not *imagine*
what it meant; only thing I could think of was there might
be some new preacher at Llangennith: it never struck me it
might have anything to do with a vessel ashore. However I
soon perceived the rocket apparatus on the lower road, so I
saw at once the meaning of it. A steamer, 2000 tons,
'Marshal Keith' from Dieppe to Llanelly had stuck on a
sand bank opposite Broughton Bay. As I met the people I
said I might as well go home! It being Sunday and there
being no little excitement here, everybody, men, women —
even Hopkins — and all the children were there. I
officiated in an almost empty church. Well, the said
steamship as the tide rose got off all right, so all the people
returned home like, in a manner, bad pennies! It is very
odd but that sort of thing so often happens on a
Sunday . . . I took that beautiful walk a day or two ago,

round by Mewslade to the cliff opposite the head.
Wonderful rocks.
Yr aff F JPL

During the winter of 1897/8 there was keen anticipation at the Rectory when it became known that Loftus and Tiny were expecting a child around the end of March. Annette had been ill and there was doubt whether she would be fit enough to go and manage the house during Tiny's confinement. In those days confinements were much more risky affairs than they are today and the mother was treated as more or less of an invalid for quite a long time before and after the birth. It was arranged that Rebecca would go and look after Tiny's household, and on the 23rd of February she set off for London. May and Flora, for the first time ever, were left in charge at the Rectory. Family letters tell vividly enough what happened next. First the Rector, writing on the 28th:

> My dear R
> Yours just recd : . . . I will take care of the paper you
> sent; of course it is not in my power to send any money
> until I receive that remittance from Mr Bentfield, but the
> moment I do I will send you some. I should hope Aunt
> Lucas' account of Charles' health is either somewhat
> mistaken or at all events exaggerated. The collection at
> Llangennith last afternoon (Church Building Society) was
> 3/9½. I will add 2½d that will make 4/–. This with Rhos 6/3
> makes 10/3 a great deal better than nothing. Caroline is
> doing her best to get something but it is uphill work.
> You should certainly while 'in town' see or hear
> something entertaining. Tiny seems most nobbit. I miss you
> very much; house seems very odd without you. You must
> miss fussing at that everlasting wardrobe. Last evening I
> read two of Wesley's sermons. I am going through them at
> the rate of two every Sunday evening. They are of course
> exceptionally fine.
> Yr aff JPL
> How comfortably you 'made your passage'. Cat caught
> large rat!

Flora wrote the same day. She was 20 years old.

> My dearest Mother
> It was very nice to hear from you this morning and I
> suppose *we* shall have a letter tomorrow. Father talks about
> you all day and seems to miss you awfully. He is always
> making funny little characteristic speeches about you —
> very complimentary ones! It is very dull without you but
> May and I have such heaps to do. What with household

things and Minnie's clothes & that never ending wash.
However we get through it quite comfortably and Minnie
has been very good. May is going to tell you all about the
boys' singing class. You would have been amused to see
them all come trooping in. We have not had so many since
Tottenham went. That wretched 'Mrs Halfpenny Street'
never came down yesterday afternoon, so I had to stay at
home and let Minnie go which was very provoking. To-day
we are going to see Mrs H. and *talk* to her — in italics.

We are going to make a round of duty calls this
afternoon, first to Annie Taylor to get her books, then on
to the Minnie Maria children, because none of them turned
up yesterday except Margaret who came in when the names
were being called, and wept. Then we are going down
through the fields to Halfpenny Street, looking in on Mrs.
Arthur Bevan on the way, and then up to Pitton X to fetch
some butter that came on Saturday — finally we must give
Annie Taylor's books to Mrs Gibbs! Your plants are all
right. How awfully jolly you three must be together —
great fun I should think. I hope Aunt Lucas has
exaggerated about Charles. You know she is given that
way, but I do think it is very bad for him to live with her,
and it ought to be stopped.

Did Tiny like the pillow case? I think I must stop now,
dear, as May is going to write too. Father told me to send
you his love, but I see he has written. Goodbye dearest
Mother. Very much love from your devoted little daughter
Flora.
PS – the cat is flourishing and says she misses a certain lady
with a cosy little black jacket very much indeed. At present
she is fast asleep on my bed.

May added her account of the day's events — Church, Sunday
school and singing class:

My dearest Mother
I must add a line to tell you about yesterday. In the
morning there were only Lois, Jane, Annie Thomas and
Stack in the choir besides Flora and me. But the new
chants went quite correctly, though the singing sounded
somewhat weak without you and Olive!

Well, in the afternoon, as Flora says, she had to stay at
home for Minnie to go — it was very annoying but we were
obliged to let her go as it was a lovely day, and she can't go
out in the evenings now. There were 32 people at the
school. Lois, Jane and Annie Taylor represented your
class. I asked Lois to teach Flora's class, and Bevan took
the other two with his. The books were all delivered

satisfactorily to their owners except Willie Gibbs' wh. Annie Taylor didn't bring back.

In the evening ten boys came down to sing viz John Beynon, Ivor and Willie Williams, Massena, Hubert and Cecil Walters, Philip George, Willie Gibbs, William Hopkins & William Beynon ('Arm' Beynon's boy)!! I can't imagine what made the last two come. They all behaved very nicely and got on with their song well. John and Massena began to learn their alto — and they even sang the first little bit altogether with the two parts quite nicely . . .

Next, two letters from the Rector:

Rhos R 4/3/98

My dear R

I wish you many happy returns of your birthday next Sunday (63). I think there hardly ever was a person who looked so very much younger than she really is. Why, I think you might very well be taken for 40 (*not* fat but fair). For a birthday present I will give you some Flower (plant) for your garden. *What* one shall be decided. There is one very handsome Van Thal tulip out, quite perfect, & lots of crocuses; a large patch with their beautiful golden eyes or centre. But it is sure to be a backward Spring; for instance it froze last night. I see by Standard LTL left Philadelphia on the 28th ult. Well I should think he would be in London by 15th or 16th instant.

As to the new schoolmaster, I met S. Bevan in the Road & asked him what sort of a man he was (he, Bevan, the previous night attended a meeting of the school board, he still being clerk). His reply was 'a very common looking man, almost like a "going about man", and he is *terribly Welshy*'. He added: 'The Board is on the horns of a dilemma' (fine words!). For they have no one to teach the infants (about which the law is most particular) — the man himself says he can do nothing about them, only being able to attend to the senior scholars; so they have actually put such people as 'Arm' Beynon's boy to teach the infants; and the master arms them, the boys etc, with a cane, with which they sometimes hit the small children, and then the mothers rush up and attack the master! A pretty state of things. S. Bevan was directed to put up a notice at Middleton (wh he characterised as *'most ridiculous'*) to this effect: 'Wanted, a candidate to teach the infants, also to teach needlework.' So it is a regular kettle of fish! Powell is the Chairman . . .

Yr aff H JPL

Rhos R.14/3/98

My dear R

Your card just arrived! So I am actually a grand F and
you a grand M. Please give best love and congratulations to
dear Tiny . . . I called on the new schoolmaster at the
school. He is, as S. Bevan said, a singularly common
looking man, and as he had not shaved he did look like a
'going about man'. He seemed very agreeable and shook
hands with me. His home is at Carmarthen. Although
common looking he may be a clever Welshman — I
afterwards same evening met W. Powell who said the
master had excellent testimonials one from a Professor at
Cambridge who said he could teach Latin and Greek.
Powell said he had been 2½ years at Aberystwyth
Coll! . . .

Yr aff H JPL

A day or two later, Rebecca wrote happily:

Little Dene
Tuesday

My dear Husband

I am obliged to write one letter to all now dears for
though I have simply *no work* to do I fuss about in and out
of dear Tiny and Baby's room, then the Doctor comes,
then there are all sorts of odds and ends to see about . . .
Tiny and Baby getting on *splendidly*. Tiny allowed fish
today and is to begin meat to-morrow. *Standard* today tells
us that the Minnesota passed the Lizard yesterday evening
so we expect Loftus here tomorrow morning. Dear Tiny so
perfectly happy — baby is too, and gets good meals of her
natural food! Mrs Cunnington very nice and good — seems
perfectly well and does all the work leaving me only the
etceteras. Yes, the basinette is 'as good as' done. I have
snatched a free hour now and again and it will go upstairs
to-night. Mrs Cunnington says it is 'sweetly pretty', and
couldn't be nicer . . . I think the christening will be in
London after all, as Tiny will not be coming to Rhosili till
early in July, and Baby will then be four months old and
short coated. Her name is at present decided to be Mary
Valentine Loftus — very pretty I think . . .

Mrs Cunnington keeps us well supplied with *plenty* of
good nice food — such delicious fried fish for supper!
Hope Minnie is all right again and that you three dears are
quite well. Tell me in your next if you are. Now I *must* go.
Your ever devoted wife and mother. XXX.

But all was not well at the Rectory. On March 19th May wrote to
her mother:

My dearest Mother

Very many thanks for all your letters, dear. Father has
not been very well the last three days (but is now much
better). It began as his chills always do with a cough and no
appetite. I tried at once to persuade him to send for the
Doctor but he would not do so until today when he
consented to have him. We telegraphed and he came this
morning. He stayed in the dining room with Father for a
long time and they had quite a little gossip together. He
says he must be careful for a few days and keep in a warm
room & and has given him some medicine. He says he
should not call it even a slight attack of influenza, but an
influenza chill. We are doing all we possibly can to take
care of him so *please do not worry about it,* dear. He seems
decidedly better since Dr R came, and has had some gruel
and a glass of wine . . . He had a fire in his room last night
and is to again tonight. I can't imagine how he got it. The
only thing I can think of is that he stood in the garden
some time in his little coat watching Thomas sowing seeds.

It began on Wednesday afternoon, but he would not let
me write to tell you before . . . Flora has just come in from
the dining room exclaiming 'Father seems ever so much
better!' So now dear please write and tell us you are not
anxious. Dr R is coming again in a day or two.

Yrs ever, May

On receiving this letter Rebecca came hurrying home, and it was
as well that she did so, for the Rector became rapidly worse.
Bronchitis was diagnosed, and probably he developed pneumonia,
for which in those days there was little the Doctor could do.
Rebecca reached home late on Sunday 21st March. The Rector
was conscious, and seemed unaware of the gravity of his illness.
Rebecca was able to tell him all about his granddaughter. He died
the following evening.

Four days later came the Rector's last journey from the Rectory
to Rhosili, carried on the bearers' shoulders, slowly and rather
awkwardly along the rough path. The family followed one by one
in deep mourning. It was a raw cold day, with a feel of snow in the
air. The group of mourners at the Churchyard gate watched the
little procession picking its way round Rolling Tor, forlorn against
the brown hillside, under a grey sky and flanked by the empty sea.

Even before the funeral Rebecca had taken the inevitable
decision. The Rectory would soon be needed for a new incumbent.
She had hardly any money. Loftus and Tiny were in Hampstead,
also Charles who was in need of a proper home. London was a

likely place for the girls to find congenial work. So the family moved to Hampstead, and within a few weeks Rebecca had left Rhosili, never to return. Within a year of his father's death Charles married his cousin Mary Matthews, and Rebecca and the girls moved into a flat.

Before long they were in their final home, 3 Snowdon Mansions, Gondar Gardens. This was a first floor flat, known in the family as '3 Snow'. Gondar Gardens was a road off Fortune Green, lined

John Richards, Parish Clerk of Rhosili, c.1895.

with terraces of small villas and three storey flats. It was quiet, with no traffic except the occasional horse and cart, errand boys on bicycles, and sometimes a man playing a barrel organ. The sitting room faced south and was filled with family bric-a-brac, and a huge glass fronted cabinet taking up most of one wall and containing the family china. 'Grandma and the aunties' as I came to know them, seemed to spend their days in this room. There were plants growing in pots and bowls in the window. There was, I think, a gas fire, but the room usually felt chilly. Behind the sitting room was a long cold dark passage with some tiny bedrooms leading off it, their windows giving on to blank brick walls. At the end of the passage was a bathroom and a very small kitchen with a rudimentary gas cooker. The kitchen faced north and enjoyed a panoramic view over Hampstead cemetery. Here at 3 Snow,

William Morgan of Rhosili, c.1896.

Rebecca lived with her memories. She cherished many keepsakes, family letters, and locks of children's hair. Letters from Rhosili people were specially treasured. One such was from John Richards the Parish Clerk, written soon after the Rector's death. He lived at the Green.

> Dear Mrs Lucas and family
>   I hope these few feeble lines will find all of you in the best health . . . The surveyor was hear last week. I was with him all over the premises he had a great deal of booking which you will have a copy of. I pointed out all the renovation that had been done by dear Mr Lucas such as the garden walls, new stable and pigstye, and many other things. I could not have explained more for any friend. I do not know for that I have any greater freinds than the whole family has been to me . . . I sees it very lonely hear without you your passing hear by our house was so frequent that is how I misses you so much and on Sundays I cannot avoid looking to Rolling Tor to see dear Mr Lucas coming round as I have seen him thousands of times . . .

When Flora and Tottenham returned to Rhosili for a visit many years later Rebecca wrote to them:

> Your letters are *intensely* interesting to me — the very next best thing to being there myself — even better I think! For there would be too great a touch of sadness to think of the loss of the dear ones laid to rest in the Churchyard. But it is *a beautiful spot to rest in* until the joyful Resurrection Morn! . . . *I love dear Rhosili where we spent so many happy years* and the dear people were so kind to me.

Rebecca died in 1930 at the age of 95. One small tribute to the Rector came too late for any of his children to hear of it, but I think they would have felt that it reflected a family tradition. One of the maids at the Rectory remembered, in her old age, her days of service there. 'Parson Lucas,' she said speaking with great emphasis, 'was a Gentleman — the *real* — the *thorough*.'

11

The Pirates of Porteynon

To people who write about Gower the Lucases of the Salthouse at Porteynon are irresistible. John Lucas, pirate, smuggler and outlaw; his descendant, another John, who died of grief when his ships and the Salthouse itself were destroyed in a famous storm; and those later Lucases fighting in the churchyard at Cheriton; they all have a place in Gower folklore. Their stories are found in a wide range of Gower literature, from the august pages of *Archaeologia Cambrensis* to the popular pamphlets stacked on the counters of tourist shops, among the love spoons and the Welsh dolls.

Where do these stories come from and what is their historical basis? One might suppose that like so much local history they are traditional stories handed down through generations of Gower folk; but this does not seem to be the case. They can almost certainly be traced to a single source, a document known as the Lucas Annotation no. 1. This purports to be a commentary on the pedigree of the Porteynon branch of the family, prepared by the Rev Dr J. H. Spry during the 1830s in connection with a family lawsuit over the ownership of property. It traces the 'family tree' from the 15th century to 1826 and it was submitted, so the document would have us believe, to the Recorder of Norwich, the Honourable Robert Alderson, who was to act as arbitrator. Alderson was in fact the Recorder of Norwich from 1826 to 1831, and died in 1833.

Before looking more closely at the history of the Annotation I will quote those parts of it which have been most used by later writers. These are only short extracts from a rambling and obscure document of some 6000 words which refers to over 100 members of the family and to over 40 places in west Gower, and in which the conclusion is reached that the Porteynon Lucases, represented in the 19th century by Richard Lucas and his descendants, are the senior male branch of the family better known as Lucas of Stouthall. The topography is accurate and some of the genealogy is correct.

The peculiarities of style and spelling may be judged from the extracts which follow. John Lucas the so-called pirate certainly existed. He was probably born around 1510, the son of David Lucas of Reynoldston. As we saw in Chapter 1 David had three sons of whom John was probably the eldest. He went to Porteynon instead of inheriting his father's property in Reynoldston, and if he was indeed the eldest son this might be evidence that his father had disinherited him. The names of John's children and his two wives are known, but otherwise we know nothing of him except what we are told in the Annotation. His descendant, whom I will call 'John the Paint' is uncorroborated outside the pages of the Annotation, where he appears seven generations after John the Pirate, so one might expect a gap of about 200 years to separate them. If the account of the fight in Cheriton churchyard is correct, this took place in the year when Richard Gorton of Burry Green was High Sheriff of Glamorgan, which was 1770. Several of the people mentioned in the Cheriton affair are historical, but the events described are uncorroborated. First, then, the story of John the Pirate:

> In course of blood and primogeniture, John Lucas would remain at Stouthall in the mansion house, for his father, David Lucas, made never a disposition. But early in his career, John Lucas incurred a spirit wild and lawless, albeit a young man 'of fine and bolde front, and very comely in the eye, and brave like a lion, but lawless and 'of fierce and ungovernable violence', and he left his father at Stouthall, and went to divers strange countries, 'engaging his handes in much violations of all laws, but always for our lord the King'. But 'after nine year, withall yet a younge man', he returned to his father in Stout Hall. His father thereupon reconciled him, 'and provided him with a portion and estate, and built him up a residence at Porth-Eynon, yclept Ye Salte House, upon taking to wife Jane, daughter to John Grove, Gentleman, Paviland, a family and place aforetime of great circumstance therein, but extinct at present writing. But it had a poor effect upon the young man, for he soon set to making a 'greate stronghold of Ye Salte House, with the battlement and walls whereof all round, reached even unto the clift and the rocks', on the edge of wild part of fore-shore near unto Porth-Eynon, and storing said stronghold with arms, and also rebuilded and repaired another stronghold called Kulverd Hall near thereunto, in the rocks, and rendered both inaccessible, save for passage thereunto through the clift'.

He also conected the two strongholds by a passage 'under the ground, whereof no man was tolde the mouthe thereof'. He became outlaw., engaged in smuggling matters, 'succoured ye pirates and ye French smugglers, and rifled ye wrecked ships and forced mariners to serve him.' He repelled all attempts to dislodge him. In these unlawful pursuits he was assisted by George ap Eynon of Brinefield, and Robert de Skurlege, and band of lawless young men gathered round them, and over them they exercised severe authority, 'even jus vitae nescisque.' It was by their aid he extended said stronghold, called The Salte House, and rebuilded the Kulverd Hall as aforementioned, and rewarded his men 'by dividing to them the spoiles, and maintaining the poor in the country rounde.' In later life he settled unto a lawful life, and thereafter abandoned Kulverd Hall, and partly dismantled his mansion, called The Salte House, so called because 'the outer battlements thereof was washed by ye salte water at flow of ye waves.'

On the body of Jane Grove, daughter to John Grove, Paviland, aforementioned, there was issue one son, Philip Lucas. On death of his father (notorious John Lucas of The Salte House), Philip Lucas and his wife Joan of Essex went from The Great House, Hortown, taking themselves unto the patrimonial mansion, The Salte House, Porth-Eynon, his mother going into the Great House, Hortown, the Dooer house, and this custom prevailed in The Salte House branch of the Lucas family many generations.

The next extract from the Annotation tells the story of the destruction of the Salt House, and the last John Lucas to live there, John the Paint, seven generations after the time of John the Pirate.

. . . After his wife Mary was dead said John Lucas of The Salte House found on land which was his in Porth-Eynon 'a vein or deposit of painte mineral', and employed men to dig therefor to the great well being and benefit to himself and to the men, and he possessed much wealth in moneys, and did buy skiffes at Swainsey and Bristol to bear ye painte mineral away, to number of five, from near to ye Salte House which was his from his fore-fathers, across the seas unto Apeldor and to coasts upon the high seas to Britain Very and Ogmoore and Nash and Kardiffe and even unto Bristol.' Teste said Gabriel Powell Gentleman, excerpt in record. On occasion of a cargo to Kardiffe 'ye skiffe was throwed ashore in great storm in a coast place called Nashe, on coast of Co. Glamorgan. Dispute thereupon arose; for much of the paint was claimed in foreshore by one Carne.' On news reaching John Lucas at

The Salte House, 'he gathered his men together into four
skiffes and went unto Nashe and wrung paymente away
from said Carne, which he got at Court of Llanfihangel and
was thereafter lodged by said Carne, and before he
returned to Ye Salte House he took to wife there one Mary
Seys, and thereby did grant gint and niddomee of said
moneys.'

Said John Lucas of the Salte House however, 'when nigh
unto death was rid of all the skiffes in one night of great
storm on Crowders Kay and Sky Sea and Uvertown Mare,
whereby he was rid of much wealth and patrimony thereby;
and ye painte mineral was after carried by skiffes that did
come from Apeldor but not his skiffes.' . . . 'and of grief
thereat said John Lucas bursted and was dead and was laid
in earth as he gave commandment, near unto ye bank of
sande beyond his mansion of Ye Salte House where he had
builded a road for ye painte to be put on ye skiffes; and ye
same dreadful night a bolt did come upon Ye Salte House,
his mansion, and ye sea broke ye battlement thereof and
tore it even unto ye great clift, and so was not to be lived
in more, whereof Mary his spouse and John his son
journeyed unto the Great House, Hortown, and all they
had and their goods was carried for many days by all men
and women and children for they was well beloved by all
men.'

The last of these extracts from the Annotation is about the fight
in Cheriton churchyard between the Stouthall Lucases and their
Porteynon cousins, then living at the Great House, Hortown; and
how the great grandson of John the Paint came to marry Mary
Gordon of Burry Green:

John Lucas, of The Great House, Hortown, made claim by
right of the first wife of his grandsire and kinswoman
Mary, daughter to John Lucas, of Stout Hall, as aforetime
is mentioned, to close of land at Cherrytown, whither and
his son, John Lucas, he journeyed with many men to force
possession thereof. The claim was 'repulsed' by his kinsman
John Lucas, of Stout Hall, who followed him with many
men thereunto. A like claim was made thereupon by John
Lucas, the younger of The Great House, Hortown, in right
of his mother Catherine Lucas, daughter as aforesaid of
Henry Lucas, of Townsend, and was supported therein by
said Henry Lucas, of Townsend, and claim proven and
admitted in yard of the Church of Cherrytown. Thereupon
ensued great disturbance and blood shed in said yard of
Church, and many supporters of John Lucas, of Stout Hall,
'thereupon was throwed into the waters of Bury and
thereupon fled, and was pursued through the woods of

Cherrytown and took sanctuary in Stowne Mill,' wherein 'John Lucas, of The Great House, Hortown, his son John and his kinsman Henry Lucas, of Townsend, and their men laid seige thereunto. Thereupon messengers sent in great haste unto George Beynon and Richard Gordon, High Sheriff, Co. Glamorgan. Said George Beynon and Richard Gordon came thereunto with their men and armed, and they raised the seige; and couzened said John Lucas, of The Great House, Hortown, and his son John with them, and before they returned to Hortown said Richard Gordon gave unto John Lucas the younger, of The Great House, Hortown, Mary, daughter, to said Richard Gordon to wife.'

NOTA. – The wife of the annotator was eye witness to the contending between the Lucases in the churchyard of Cherrytown from the window of her father's residence, the Great House, Cherrytown hard by, her father, John Williams, clericus, Master of Arts, then Rector of Cherrytown and she bound in blood to the parties, her mother was Anne Lucas, daughter to Richard Lucas of Peartree, cousin in blood of contending parties. The scene is before her, and she sees again her kinsman John Lucas of the Great House, Hortown and Porth-Eynon, very stalwart and powerful, standing upon the tomb with his father behind him calling unto their followers around them, forcing their kinsman and his men over the banks even into the river, whence they ran along the bed thereof under the ford. John Lucas the younger saying unto her as he pursued, 'Uncle is in church, Anne, don't cry', whereby his assurance of safety of her father, who, being clergy, he locked in the church, it being offensive to shed blood in sight of clergy.

The earliest reference to the Annotation which I have been able to discover is a letter dated 22nd July 1908 from a Mr Isacke of Sutton Coldfield near Birmingham to the Gower historian the Rev J. D. Davies at Llanmadoc, enclosing a copy of the document. Isacke seems to have been a collector of Welsh pedigrees. He gives no clue to the source of the Annotation which he says has been lent to him and speaks vaguely of 'the record from London'. It is plain that he has no personal knowledge of Gower since he asks Davies whether such places as Llangennith and Stouthall 'still exist'. Davies found the document 'strangely worded and obscure', a verdict with which few will quarrel; but he later concluded it was 'of great value' and proposed to use it in his final volume dealing with the history of Porteynon, which remained uncompleted at the time of his death in 1912.

The next appearance of the Annotation is a printed version described as a precis, circulated in about 1910, the typography of which is consistent with the work of a provincial printer of that time. It was accompanied by a circular bearing no name or address and referring to a forthcoming work *County Families of England and Wales* to be published in ten volumes of about 300 pages each, 'in style of the accompanying specimen pages'. The volumes were to be arranged 'on a territorial basis', and the price was to be eight guineas net. In fact no such work was ever published. The Annotation bears no resemblance to specimen pages of such a book, and it is hard to imagine that any publisher would have gone to the expense of producing for publicity purposes such a lengthy and elaborate document relating to one branch of an unimportant family; still less would he have circulated it anonymously.

It is surprising to find that the Annotation, with such a dubious provenance, was taken seriously, but such was the case. It was launched into Gower history on the afternoon of the 12th August 1920, when the members of the Cambrian Archaeological Society meeting in Swansea concluded their day's excursion at Porteynon. After clambering round Porteynon Point in the rain they assembled in the rocky gulley at the foot of Culver Hole. A ladder was produced and their local secretary Mr Percy Williams climbed into the lowest of the stone archways and read a prepared address. Giving as his source a new work on County Families — although he admitted he had not had access to the work itself — Mr Williams quoted at length from the Annotation the stories of John the Pirate, John the Paint and the fight in Cheriton churchyard. It seems from the report of the proceedings in the Society's journal he accepted the document as a true historical record, and if any of the assembled members had doubts they are not mentioned.

During the ensuing 50 years most writers on Gower history have used these stories at one time or another. The late Mr Horatio Tucker, whose *Gower Gleanings* is a classic of its kind, was enthusiastic. 'I do really think' he wrote in 1950, 'that the facts given in (the Annotation) are authentic. The dates are all exactly confirmed from other sources . . . Everything ties up with other Gower history.' In his article *The Salt House Story* which appeared in the *Swansea Evening Post* in 1950 and was reprinted in *Gower Gleanings* the following year, Tucker re-tells the Annotation stories with one important addition: he ascribes the destruction of the Salt

House to the 'Great Storm' of 1703.

Tucker's version of the Salt House story seems to have been the basis of most of the articles and pamphlets which have appeared since 1950, but a further elaboration followed and is repeated in Mr Wynford Vaughan-Thomas's *Portrait of Gower* published in 1976. The Annotation tells us that the Pirate in his later years 'settled unto a lawful life' but Mr Vaughan-Thomas has him 'passing on the piracy business' to his son Philip, and his descendants at the Salt House continuing their criminal activities until a 'faint deviation into legality' at the end of the 17th century, after which the Great Storm brought the affair to its dramatic climax. With the Salt House story so firmly entrenched in Gower annals, it is still not too late in the day to test it against contemporary sources. Having done that we can go on to consider whether the document itself contains any clues as to its true provenance.

There are some things obviously wrong with the Annotation, such as the fact that there are too many generations of Porteynon Lucases to fit into the time available, but this does not necessarily invalidate the stories which have the appearance of being quoted from some earlier and unspecified source. The fight in Cheriton churchyard, to take the last story first, cannot easily be disproved, and the recollection of Anne Williams has such a ring of truth about it that I was for some time persuaded that it was founded on fact. Yet, the surrounding circumstances make the story improbable. John Lucas of Stouthall was in 1770 a widower aged 66 with only one surviving child, a boy of 11. From what we know of him, he seems to have been a careful and frugal landowner and a conscientious Justice of the Peace; hardly the sort of man to be involved in a brawl of this kind. Anne Williams, who later married Dr Spry the so-called Annotator, was the youngest of the three daughters of the Rev John Williams, Rector of Cheriton. The evidence of tombstones and parish records is not conclusive, but it seems likely that Anne was not born until 1771, and so could not have witnessed events in 1770. As for the story about young John Lucas of Horton marrying Mary daughter of Richard Gordon of Burry Green who was sheriff in 1770, this Richard Gordon's will is in the National Library. He died in 1780 and in his will, which mentions by name two daughters, a sister and five grandchildren, there is no mention of a daughter Mary or Lucas son-in-law. This is hardly surprising since according to the parish records young John Lucas of Horton was already married in 1770. His wife was Ruth Bevan, not Mary

Gordon. John Williams's map of Penrice parish in 1783 shows John Lucas living at the house which is now the Post Office, not the Great House which was then let to Samuel Bevan and unconnected with the farm let to the Lucases.

Even more remarkable is the fact that there seems to have been no local tradition in Cheriton about the affair, and neither J. D. Davies in his *History of Cheriton Parish* published in 1879 nor C. D. Morgan in his *Wanderings in Gower* published in 1862 make any mention of this or any other tale in the Annotation. It is hard to believe that these two Gowermen, born and bred in west Gower, would have missed a good story, particularly Davies who was Rector of Llanmadoc from 1860 and Cheriton from 1867, and writes at length about the Rev John Williams who was Rector of Cheriton at the date of the supposed fight. Miss Nell Thomas, formerly schoolmistress at the Hill School who, and whose parents before her, lived all their lives in Cheriton, told me a few years ago that the story of the fight was unknown to her.

To return to the Salt House, it is known that in the 18th century the Clements family were living at the Salt House cottages which are said to have been built on or near the ruins of the old mansion. A few years ago Mr Michael Gibbs in a lecture at Swansea's Royal Institution fired a well aimed shot across the pirate's bows when he drew attention to the evidence of Isaac Hamon of Bishopston and the Hearth Tax return of the year 1670. Hamon in his survey of Gower written for Edward Lhuyd in 1697 says of Porteynon 'here was about 40 years agoe a salt house near the key of Porthynon'. He says nothing about a paint mine, which did exist in the village for a time in the 19th century. If it had been there in the 1690s one would have expected Hamon to mention it. The Hearth Tax returns show that in 1670 the principal house in the village, with four hearths, was occupied by Francis Clement. No Lucas is mentioned. Does this mean that the destruction of the Salt House happened 40 years before Hamon wrote? Not necessarily, because the truth of the matter is that the Salt House was so named not because its battlements were washed by 'ye salte water at flow of ye waves', but because as early as Elizabethan times it was used for the manufacture of salt by panning the sea water. We read in Sir Edward Stradling's late 16th century letters of a 'bote of salte arryvinge at Aberthaw (Swansea) out of Portheynon'. Hamon's comment may simply mean that this salt trade had ceased 'about 40 years agoe'.

However we can go further back in our search for Lucases at the Salt House. In the Penrice and Margam collections of MSS in the National Library of Wales is a survey of the manor of Porteynon made between 1627 and 1636. Here we do find a Lucas but he is not at the Salt House. He is George Lucas a yeoman farmer with a house and 18 acres at Overton. If in about the year 1630 we had ventured out towards Porteynon Point we would indeed have found the Salthouse, then inhabited not by a lawless crew of Lucases but by the unromantic figure of Em Gribble, an elderly widow. The survey records that by a Lease dated 7th October 1598 one John Griffith, his wife Em Gribble and their son Frank took a lease for lives of 'one house neere Porteinons key comonly called the saullt house and the ould walles with the little parcel of ground on the backside thereunto belonging.' The rent was ten shillings per annum with the usual manorial incidents in addition. This seems rather a high rent for a house with hardly any land, so very likely Em carried on the salt panning business, and paid a business rent. She alone of the family was still alive at the date of the survey.

We have now arrived back almost at the time of the 'pirate'. This John Lucas who, as we saw, was the son of David Lucas of Reynoldston, was twice married. By his second wife Jane Grove he had a son Philip who married Joan Sussex — not as the Annotation would have us believe Joan of Essex who connects so conveniently with the East Anglian tradition, and whose father lived so romantically on the Burry Holmes, or so the Annotation tells us. The 'pirate' had a second son Richard who was a yeoman farmer living in Llandewi parish and died in 1601. Richard bequeathed his residuary estate to his brother Philip. The George Lucas mentioned in the survey was very likely Philip's son. He too was a yeoman farmer and when he died his farm stock and household goods were valued for probate at £23–6–8. John Lucas 'the pirate' still eludes us and we cannot say for certain what manner of man he was. But it is already evident that most of the Salt House story is a work of fiction, the likelihood seems to be that he was just another of the local farmers.

The question who wrote the Annotation, and why, presents a fascinating field for enquiry, and I do not claim to know the answer. The genealogy is a mixture of the accurate and the fanciful. Much of the language is confused, ungrammatical, larded with archaic words and pseudo-legal jargon. It purports to have been written by Dr J. H. Spry as evidence in a family lawsuit. This Dr Spry was a friend of two late 18th century Gower parsons whom we have already met, Williams of Cheriton and Collins of Oxwich, and he married Anne Williams, the parson's youngest daughter. He was a man of learning, much involved in theological controversy. He had livings in Birmingham and London where he became one of the notable churchmen of his day. It is hardly conceivable that he could have written anything so confused as the Annotation as serious evidence in a lawsuit. We must conclude therefore that the Annotation is not what it purports to be. Yet the stories woven in to this clumsy document, although fictitious, are lively and cleverly told, and have a strong 'literary' quality. John the Pirate 'very comely in the eye and brave like a lion'; John the Paint who 'gathered his men together into four skiffes and went unto Nashe and wrung payment away from said Carne'; the description of the great storm; and the later John Lucas 'very stalwart and powerful, standing upon the tomb' with his reassurance to little Anne Williams: 'Uncle is in church, Anne, don't cry.' This is not the work of a rustic scribe but of an educated man, an author well versed in the romantic school. What is the explanation of this inconsistency, the muddle and the good writing? May it be a case of dual authorship, with the good stories adapted to the genealogy by a later less skilful hand? If we start looking for an author of the stories with the necessary literary qualifications, knowledge of Gower and connection with the Lucases, there is a candidate ready to hand.

The Rev William Lucas Collins (1815–87) was the son of John Collins, Rector of Ilston, and Elizabeth his wife, who was a granddaughter of Richard Lucas of Peartree. After graduating from Jesus College, Oxford in 1838, W. L. Collins took Holy Orders and in 1840 became Rector of Cheriton, a post which he held for 27 years. Also in 1840 he married Frances Wood a sister of Colonel Wood. In 1867 Collins resigned the living of Cheriton to become Rector of Lowick in Northamptonshire where he died in 1887. Sir George Leveson Gower, who as a young man was a pupil of Collins, remembers him as a Churchman of the 'High and Dry' school, a keen cricketer, an elegant and accurate scholar, and a man of the world gifted with a ready wit and a sense of humour. Collins was a literary man, a close friend of Anthony Trollope, who wrote the last of his novels at Lowick Rectory. In his twenties Collins was already contributing to *Blackwoods Magazine* which he continued to do throughout his life. He edited a popular series of books entitled *Ancient Classics for English Readers* and wrote several of them. He also wrote a two volume historical romance *The Luck of Ladysmede* published in 1860, a tale of medieval England in which the antiquarian atmosphere is laid on thickly. Did he also perhaps write some romantic tales about his Gower forebears? It is curious that the Annotation concludes with the following postscript which just might be more than another red herring:

> Nota post annotationes. Calamo William Lucas Collins,
> Master of Arts, Rector of Lowick, Canon (honoris causa)
> of Peterboro'. The said Richard Lucas was thereafter laid
> to rest . . . and thereupon lapsed and came unto an end
> which had never happened theretofore the males of the
> senior line of Lucas, notable and distinct through over 400
> years as heretofore of verity appeareth. Thus aforesaid
> three daughters be sole living in first blood direct
> impeccable. And so thenceforth partus sequitur ventrem.
> Amen.

If we are right about dual authorship then, whoever wrote the stories be it William Lucas Collins or someone else, we still have to find the enthusiastic genealogist, someone so strongly motivated as to have composed the document in its present form and to have had it printed. There is one significant pointer. The Annotation maintains, even to the extent of having it printed in heavy type, that in the 1830s the surviving senior male representative of the Lucases was Richard Lucas of Porteynon, and not as most people would have supposed, Colonel John Nicholas Lucas of Stouthall. It was one of Richard Lucas' descendants, the late Miss Eleanor Lucas-Hughes, who treasured a copy of the Annotation which is longer than the printed version, and may be the original of which the printed version is a precis.

I believe the answer to the puzzle probably lies in the 19th century family pride which so often turned to snobbishness, and in the jealousies to which this gave rise. The Stouthall family in the 19th century were 'County' and they let people know it. Richard Lucas of Porteynon and his children were not; and if they met old Colonel Lucas or his daughter Mrs Wood they would be expected to touch their caps and say 'Good Morning, Sir', 'Good Morning Ma'am'. Towards the end of the century more came to be known about Gower pedigrees. It became evident from such sources as G. T. Clark's *Genealogies of Glamorgan*, and the William Bennett pedigrees that it was probably the eldest son of David Lucas, and so the senior branch of the family, which became established at

Porteynon in the 16th century. If the grandchildren of Richard Lucas of Porteynon could prove descent from that first John Lucas, son of David, the tables would be neatly turned; Jack would not only be as good as his master, he would have gone one better. Suppose the 'Collins' stories came to hand, what an opportunity for someone to complete the Porteynon pedigree, perhaps supplying some missing links in a legal sounding way, and then send it round — a nice touch this — as part of a County Family History.

This is guesswork and may be wide of the mark. But in case it sounds far-fetched to suppose that anyone would go to the trouble and expense of producing a complicated document like the Annotation to give credence to a rather meaningless claim of precedence, let the representatives of the two branches of the family speak for themselves. First the Rev J. P. Lucas of Rhosili, writing in about 1890 at a time when he was the eldest living male member of the Stouthall branch:

> A word about Lucas of Stouthall. First I must *protest most strongly* against the *absurd* account of the family given in Glamorgan pedigrees by Mr Clark; when he entered upon the matter this is what he did, he took as it were a net and gathered together all the people of that name in Gower and assumed they were all one family, than which nothing could be more ridiculous. Of all the Lucases he named not half of them were the same as Lucas of Stouthall; for instance Lucas of Porteynon were entirely a different people. His account altogether is entirely misleading. Lucas of Stouthall is descended from the very ancient and historical family of Lucas of Essex; they came in with the Conqueror . . .

Next Mrs Ruth Harris representing Porteynon, upon whose tombstone in Reynoldston churchyard are inscribed the following words:

> In loving memory of Ruth Beynon Harris of Brynfield Hall in this Parish born March 9th 1833 died October 3rd 1900. Granddaughter of Richard Lucas Esquire with whom terminated the lineal male line of the senior (or Porteynon) branch of the family of Lucas of Stouthall.

We may not have found the author of the Annotations; and the old walls at the Salt House remain as mysterious as ever. But have we at last scuppered the pirates of Porteynon? John Lucas is a Gower folk hero, and perhaps one should keep an open mind. My search for the Salt House Lucases made me think of that hot afternoon in June 1894 when Parson Davies of Llanmadoc toiling up the hill to Penrice from Penny Hitch encountered a tall man in a frock coat and a wideawake hat. As Davies came nearer the man turned grey and vanished into thin air. The Rector preserved an open mind and invited the apparition through the medium of the Church Magazine to get in touch with him. In a similar spirit of enquiry I once invited any reader of the *Gower Journal* with knowledge of the pirate or his crew to get in touch with me. So far, like Parson Davies, I have been disappointed.

Ruins of the Salthouse and Cottages

The Rev Canon William Lucas Collins 1815–87.
Was he the author of the Salthouse stories?

Author's Note on Sources

The chief primary sources for this book are the correspondence, papers and title deeds in the possession of members of the family, personal recollections, and various collections of papers in the National Library in Wales. Details have had to be omitted for lack of space, but for anyone interested a supplement to the book in similar form is available from the author c/o The Book Guild Limited, Temple House, 25 High Street, Lewes, East Sussex BN7 2LU. This contains:

(1) Notes on each chapter and details of all sources used.
(2) Pedigrees of Lucas of Stouthall, Lucas of Hills, Lucas of Penmaes (the latter being descendants of Richard Lucas of Peartree), Bowen of Gurrey Manor, Wood of Stouthall, Matthews of Bedford, and a simplified pedigree of Loftus, Tottenham and Ponsonby showing the Lucas connection.
(3) A schedule of properties belonging to the Stouthall estate at various dates, also Probate inventories etc.

By way of acknowledgment I list below some of the secondary sources which I have found helpful.

Memoir of Sir Gardner Wilkinson F.R.S. by W. S. Vaux. Royal Soc. of Literature 1876.
West Gower by J. D. Davies. 4 vols. Cambrian Press 1877–94.
The Conway by John Masefield. Heinemann 1933.
The South Wales Squires by Herbert Vaughan. Methuen 1926.
The Life of T. R. Matthews by Thomas Wright. C. J. Farncombe & Sons 1934.
Transactions of Hon. Society of Cymmrodorion 1948 (H. J. Lloyd-Johnes on the Glanareth murder) 1965 (F. V. Emery on Edward Lhuyd and his correspondents) and 1968 (Lady Llanover and her circle).
National Library of Wales Journals 1955/6 and 57/8 (F. V. Emery on West Glam Farming).
Gower Society Journals 9 and 13 (Iorwerth Hughes Jones on Fairyhill); 13 (C. E. Vulliamy on Stouthall and D. H. Hey on Prosecution of felons); 17 (Phoebe Simons on Southey and B. Morris on Gower houses); 26 (F. V. Emery on clover cultivation and B. Morris on 19th century Swansea); 25–28 (Dr J. Martin on Penrice and Talbot family).
Glamorgan Gentry 1650–1770 PhD thesis by Dr J. P. Jenkins. Cambridge University Library.
Peacocks in Paradise by Elisabeth Inglis-Jones. Faber & Faber 1950.
The Crawshays of Cyfarthfa Castle by M. S. Taylor. Hale 1967.
George Owen of Henllys by B. G. Charles. National Library of Wales 1973.

Morgannwg (Journal of Glamorgan History Society) 1977 (L. Hergest on Wood family).

Pages from the history of Llandovery by A. T. Arbor-Cooke. 1975.

Clyne Castle Swansea by R. A. Griffiths. 1977.

Gower Shipwrecks by P. H. Rees. Christopher Davies 1978.

The Gower Churches by G. R. Orrin with introduction by Dr F. G. Cowley. 1979.

History of Llandovery College by W. Gareth Evans. 1981.

Royal Commission on Ancient & Historical Monuments Glamorgan Inventory. The greater houses.